D1086934

COLLECTING
BASEBALL AND
OTHER SPORTS
CARDS

Dr. James Beckett

HOUSE OF COLLECTIBLES

NEW YORK   TORONTO   LONDON   SYDNEY   AUCKLAND

Copyright © 2007 by Beckett Publications, Inc.

Important Notice: All the information, including valuations, in this book has been compiled from reliable sources, and efforts have been made to eliminate errors and questionable data. Nevertheless, the possibility of error always exists in a work of such immense scope. The publisher will not be responsible for any losses that may occur in the purchase, sale, or other transaction of items because of information contained herein. Readers who feel they have discovered errors are invited to write and inform us, so that such errors can be corrected in subsequent editions.

House of Collectibles and colophon are registered trademarks of Random House, Inc.

RANDOM HOUSE is a registered trademark of Random House, Inc.

This book is available for special discounts for bulk purchases for sales promotions or premiums. Special editions, including personalized covers, excerpts of existing books, and corporate imprints, can be created in large quantities for special needs. For more information, write to Special Markets/Premium Sales, 1745 Broadway, MD 6-2, New York, NY, 10019 or E-mail specialmarkets@randomhouse.com.

Please address inquiries about electronic licensing of any products for use on a network, in software, or on CD-ROM to the Subsidiary Rights Department, Random House Information Group, fax 212-572-6003.

Visit the House of Collectibles Web site:
www.houseofcollectibles.com.

Library of Congress Cataloging-in-Publication Data:
Beckett, James.
   Collecting baseball and other sports cards : instant expert / James Beckett.
      p. cm.
ISBN 978-0-375-72094-9
1. Sports cards—Collectors and collecting—United States. I. Title: Instant expert.   II. Title.
GV568.5.B43 2006
796.075—dc22   2005055074

Printed in the United States of America.

10 9 8 7 6 5 4 3 2 1

CONTENTS

INTRODUCTION

Let's begin with this premise: They don't make sports cards like they used to. In fact, they haven't in quite some time. These days, it's a whole different ball game, so to speak. Once little more than a childhood summertime obsession, one of America's favorite hobbies is now a much more highly refined pursuit than it was even twenty years ago, to say the least. If all you remember about collecting sports cards is the staid insipidness of the ho-hum photography and the concrete confectionery passed off as bubble gum, you might want to sit down. This book will open your eyes to a whole new and dramatically different world.

Likely gone forever are the hackneyed bike-spoke horror stories and tales of Mom "donating" our shoe-boxed collections to the local landfill while we were away at college. Mom wouldn't dare be as frivolous with today's brand of cards, with their sophisticated printing technologies and flat-out revolutionary incorporation of authentic, game-worn memorabilia and player autographs.

Baseball cards today bring collectors closer to their favorite players and teams than ever before. Pieces of gum in packs have been replaced by pieces of authentic, game-worn jerseys, batting helmets, gloves, shoes, bats, bases, and baseballs; old-school facsimile autographs on trading cards have been replaced by genuine, certified autographs from the players themselves. The quality of baseball card photography is at an all-time high; the statistics and player information on the backs of the cards are as comprehensive and in-depth as ever.

Oh, and the overall selection of sports card sets? Well, that's at an all-time high, too. And baseball's no longer the only game in town. In recent years, the rising popularity of the NBA, NFL, and NHL have made basketball, football, and hockey cards increasingly essential for card collectors. Walk into your local sports card shop today, and you're likely to be either impressed or overwhelmed by the staggering amount of choices on the market. That's a big change from years past: As recently as 1980, Topps's final year as the only card maker in the business, the baseball card season essentially boiled down to one set a year, followed by an updated set at season's end to

Upper Deck logo

Topps logo

capture the significant player movement that had transpired during that season.

The two major licensed baseball card companies, Topps and Upper Deck, produce roughly forty different baseball sets a year, creating a choice-riddled industry with myriad products ranging in price from 99 cents a pack to $250 a pack (that's right, $250 a pack). The great thing about having so many options is that there's a baseball card set for virtually every taste. You can be a content collector whether you get $10 a month for allowance, get $20 a week, or earn $200,000 a year.

Therein lies what has always been the beauty of this hobby: How you collect, what you collect, and why you collect is absolutely, completely, 100 percent up to you. You can collect one sport or many; you can collect complete sets (although that's not nearly as popular as it once was; we'll get into exactly why later); you can collect your favorite player; you can collect all the players from your favorite team; you can collect only 500-Home-Run-Club members or Heisman Trophy winners. The choices are endless.

At their core, sports cards remain an extension of our individual sporting loyalties. They allow us an avenue for exhibiting our love for the home team and our devotion to our favorite players, and, more recently, a chance at finding bona fide, high-dollar pieces of history honoring the game's greatest players.

So, yes, the trading card industry has changed—a lot—since those more-innocent days gone by. Completists have given way to opportunists, creating a hobby with fewer set builders and more gold diggers. Baseball's newcomers no longer warrant only one Rookie Card; the best boast forty or fifty. Selections are plentiful, prices are higher, and the value delivered by card manufacturers at seemingly every level is at an all-time high.

But some things, perhaps the most important things, haven't changed. Sports cards are woven into the very fabric of Americana as a beloved, generation-bridging hobby shared by millions. And that's why sports cards have been around for 110 years, and why they're sure to be around for at least that many more.

Part 1

THINK AND TALK
LIKE AN EXPERT

An important part of collecting is knowing the essential terms and fundamentals that can turn any new collector into an instant expert. Part 1 introduces you to the basics of what to collect and what makes a card collectible; card collectors' lingo; buying and selling cards; advice on protecting your collection; and warnings about counterfeits.

1

WHAT TO COLLECT

Many collectors jumping into sports card collecting for the first time get overwhelmed very quickly. It's easy to be confused by all the card products out there; after all, there is a seemingly endless range of choices for all types of collectors. In choosing cards to collect, the best starting point is to know what you like. Remember: Card collectors are sports fans first. As a result, many people collect cards because they are direct links to favorite players or teams.

Favorite Players
Collecting your favorite players' cards is easy; it's a simple matter of searching for them. The top baseball stars will appear on hundreds of cards each year. The Yankees' Alex Rodriguez, for example, appeared on more than a thousand different cards in 2003 alone. It would be virtually impossible to collect every one, but again, don't feel overwhelmed. Just collect what you like. You can choose a particular brand on which to focus, or aim for cards from particular seasons or stages in a player's career.

Teams

Many collectors follow certain teams. Although not every type of card or set includes every player on every team, you can bet that the most popular players on every team will have plenty of cards for you to collect. Thanks to cool "combo" cards featuring multiple teammates, team collecting can be a lot of fun. Many collectors will try to collect every card in a certain set that features players from their favorite teams. Hobby shop dealers in your area should be able to help you find cards featuring certain players or teams.

Rookies

Some of the hobby's most sought-after and in-demand cards feature rookie players. Rookie Cards are the driving force behind the baseball, football, basketball, and hockey card industries. Why are they so desirable? Because they are the first cards produced featuring certain players. Star players will appear on thousands of cards produced throughout their careers, but will appear on only a finite number of Rookie Cards. Today, many Rookie Cards are available long before a player takes his first at bat or hurls his first fastball in the majors. And most of today's rookies will have multiple Rookie Cards. Vintage Rookie Cards (pre-1980) are also highly collected. Below are some of the most popular and most collected Rookie Cards of all time in the four major sports (with their approximate values):

Baseball:

1948 Bowman Stan Musial #36 ($800)

1949 Leaf Leroy "Satchel" Paige #8 ($12,000)

1949 Leaf Jackie Robinson #79 ($1,500)

1951 Bowman Mickey Mantle #253 ($8,000)

1951 Bowman Willie Mays #305 ($2,500)

1954 Topps Hank Aaron #128 ($1,800)

1955 Topps Roberto Clemente #164 ($2,000)

1963 Topps Pete Rose #537 ($1,000)

1968 Topps Nolan Ryan/Jerry Koosman #177 ($500)

1969 Topps Reggie Jackson #260 ($300)

1980 Topps Rickey Henderson #482 ($50)

1982 Topps Cal Ripken #21 ($50)

1985 Topps Mark McGwire #401 ($30)

1987 Fleer Barry Bonds #604 ($50)

1989 Upper Deck Ken Griffey Jr. #1 ($50)

1993 SP Derek Jeter #279 ($60)

1994 SP Alex Rodriguez #15 ($100)

2001 Bowman Chrome Albert Pujols #340 ($3,200)

2001 SPx Ichiro Suzuki #150 ($800)

2001 Leaf Limited Mark Prior #307 ($100)

2002 Bowman Chrome David Wright #358 ($350)

2003 SPx Hideki Matsui #161 ($400)

2003 SPx Delmon Young #382 ($450)

2004 Bowman Chrome Felix Hernandez #345 ($175)

Football:

1935 National Chicle Bronko Nagurski #34 ($5,000)

1948 Leaf Sammy Baugh #34 ($600)

1950 Topps Felt Backs Joe Paterno #64 ($1,800)

1957 Topps Bart Starr #119 ($450)

1957 Topps Johnny Unitas #138 ($450)

1954 Topps
Hank Aaron
#128

1957 Topps Paul Hornung #151 ($400)

1958 Topps Jim Brown #62 ($450)

1965 Topps Joe Namath #122 ($1,600)

1971 Topps Terry Bradshaw #156 ($200)

1976 Topps Walter Payton #148 ($250)

1981 Topps Joe Montana #216 ($150)

1984 Topps John Elway #63 ($80)

1984 Topps Dan Marino #123 ($80)

1986 Topps Jerry Rice #161 ($80)

1989 Score Barry Sanders #257 ($40)

1989 Score Troy Aikman #270 ($30)

1990 Score Supplemental Emmitt Smith #101T ($60)

1991 Stadium Club Brett Favre #94 ($50)

1993 SP Drew Bledsoe #9 ($30)

1998 SP Authentic Peyton Manning #14 ($800)

1998 SP Authentic Randy Moss #18 ($250)

2000 SP Authentic Tom Brady #118 ($800)

2001 SP Authentic Michael Vick #91 ($1,500)

2003 SP Authentic Byron Leftwich #269 ($500)

2004 SP Authentic Ben Roethlisberger #213 ($750)

Basketball:

1948 Bowman George Mikan #69 ($2,500)

1957–58 Topps Bob Cousy #17 ($400)

1957–58 Topps Bill Russell #77 ($1,000)

1961–62 Fleer Wilt Chamberlain #8 ($800)

1961–62 Fleer Oscar Robertson #36 ($400)

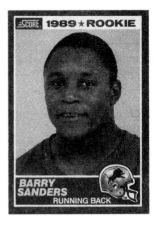

1961–62 Fleer Jerry West #43 ($500)

1969–70 Topps Lew Alcindor #25 ($350)

1970–71 Topps Pete Maravich #123 ($300)

1972–73 Topps Julius Erving #195 ($200)

1974–75 Topps Bill Walton #39 ($50)

1974–75 Topps George Gervin #196 ($40)

1980–81 Topps Larry Bird/Julius Erving/Magic Johnson #6 ($250)

1986–87 Fleer Charles Barkley #7 ($50)

1986–87 Fleer Michael Jordan #57 ($750)

1992–93 Upper Deck Shaquille O'Neal #1 ($40)

1995–96 Finest Kevin Garnett #115 ($70)

1996–97 Topps Chrome Kobe Bryant ($225)

1998–99 SP Authentic Vince Carter #95 ($150)

2002–03 SP Authentic Yao Ming #143 ($100)

2003–04 SP Authentic LeBron James #148 ($750)

2003–04 SP Authentic Dwyane Wade #152 ($500)

2004–05 SP Authentic Ben Gordon #185 ($200)

1965 Topps
Joe Namath
#122

1989 Score
Barry Sanders
#257

1986–87
Fleer
Michael
Jordan #57

Hockey:

1951–52 Parkhurst Maurice "Rocket" Richard #4 ($1,600)

1951–52 Parkhurst Gordie Howe #66 ($3,000)

1958–59 Topps Bobby Hull #66 ($3,000)

1966–67 Topps Bobby Orr #35 ($2,500)

1979–80 OPC Wayne Gretzky #18 ($900)

1984–85 OPC Steve Yzerman #67 ($125)

1985–86 OPC Mario Lemieux #9 ($200)

1986–87 OPC Patrick Roy #53 ($150)

Set Collecting

Collecting sets is one of the most ambitious goals a collector can have. Although it can be very expensive and challenging, completing a set is one of the most rewarding achievements you will ever experience as a collector.

Vintage sets are more desirable and tougher to complete than modern sets. Let's take the 1956 Topps Baseball set as an example. This set consists of 340 cards and is valued at between $5,000 and $8,000, depending on condition. Many collectors trying to complete this set will first secure the top, most expensive cards, such as the Mickey Mantle, Ted Williams, and Roberto Clemente. After adding the top cards, a smart next step is to buy the lower-priced cards in bunches—or "lots," as they are commonly dubbed. Many of these cards can be found in online auctions grouped into larger lots.

The typical modern card product can be broken down into a *base set* (basic Rookie Cards and other short prints), *parallels* (featuring designs similar to those of base cards, but with some distinctive differences), and *inserts* (special cards inserted randomly into boxes that feature special themes, designs, and various "bells and whistles"). Since almost every current card set has many parallels and rare insert cards, completing a *master set* (a group that includes one of every card in a product) is extremely difficult. However, completing a *base set* (a group consisting only of basic cards) that includes Rookie Cards is a much more attainable goal.

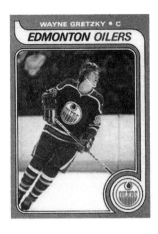

1979–80 OPC
Wayne
Gretzky #18

Topical Subset Collecting

More and more these days, the sheer amount of baseball card products on the market is forcing collectors to narrow their collecting goals, and one of the most popular ways to do that is by building what are called *topical subsets*. A topical subset is any collection in which the cards share a common thread. Some examples: cards featuring 500-Home-Run-Club members, cards featuring players who went to your college, cards featuring players from your hometown, cards featuring World Series MVPs, and cards featuring players who share your first or last name. The list goes on and on, but the greatest thing about a topical subset is that its parameters are entirely up to you.

Vintage vs Modern

We've already briefly discussed vintage and modern cards. Collectors are attracted to both for different reasons. So, what are the differences between the two? Sports card hobbyists generally consider cards produced before 1980 to be vintage cards. Being older and of lower production quality than their modern counterparts, vintage cards are more "condition sensitive," which means that they are more vulnerable to damage throughout their life. This is why graded vintage cards have become so popular. Because they were not widely considered to be collectors' items during their production days, vintage cards for the most part are more rare than most modern cards, which adds to their value. Naturally, most modern card sets focus on current players, though many baseball sets also feature some all-time greats. There are some dealers who buy and sell strictly vintage cards; however, most dealers offer both vintage and modern card selections.

2

WHAT MAKES
A CARD
COLLECTIBLE?

Many factors go into determining the value and collectibility of a card. One of the most obvious factors is the player's status. As we said before, collectors are sports fans first, so they know who the superstars are. For that reason, it's pretty easy to determine which players' cards are most valuable: A player's performance on the field directly affects the value of his cards. But a player's status is not the only factor that determines a card's value. Like any other commodity that is bought, sold, or traded in a free, unregulated market, sports cards are subject to the law of supply and demand. Generally speaking, the smaller the number of cards printed, the higher the demand for those cards.

It is important to note that card prices for a certain player may vary from region to region. For example, cards featuring New York Yankees shortstop Derek Jeter typically will sell for a higher price in the New York area than they will, say, in Arizona. So, knowing this, you can expect to pay a little more for cards featuring players in your area. This phenomenon is known in the industry as a *regional premium*.

Generally, the following factors will determine a card's value:

(1) the age of the card

(2) the number of cards printed

(3) the fame, popularity, and talent of the player featured on the card

(4) the attractiveness and popularity of the set

(5) the condition of the card

Though there may be exceptions regarding the extent to which some of these factors affect a card's value, the importance of a card's condition remains constant. Thus, if two cards are similar with respect to the first four factors listed above, then differences in the conditions of the two cards will greatly affect their relative values. Although the methodology of individual dealers and card grading companies may vary, the sports card hobby does have its own general terminology when it comes to identifying condition. Generally, the most important areas of concern are as follows:

Centering

Current centering terminology uses numbers to represent the percentage of border on either side of a card's main design. Obviously, centering is diminished in importance for borderless cards such as full-bleed photo cards.

Slightly Off-Center (60/40): A *slightly off-center* card is one that, upon close inspection, is found to have one border bigger than the opposite border. Such cards were once offensive only to purists, but now some hobbyists try to avoid cards that are anything other than perfectly centered.

Slightly off-center

Well-centered

Off-center

Badly off-center

Miscut

This 1962 Topps Hank Aaron card has a slightly rounded corner. Note that there is definite corner wear, as evidenced by the fraying, and that the corner no longer sports a sharp point.

This 1962 Topps Gil Hodges card has corner wear, but is in slightly better condition than the Aaron card. Nevertheless, some collectors might classify this Hodges corner as "slightly rounded."

Off-Center (70/30): An *off-center* card has one border that is noticeably more than twice as wide as the opposite border.

Badly Off-Center (80/20 or worse): A *badly off-center* card has virtually no border on one side of the card.

Miscut: A *miscut* card actually shows, in its larger border, part of the adjacent card from the printing sheet. Consequently, a corresponding amount of the card's own image is cut off on the opposite side.

Corner Wear

Corner wear is the most scrutinized grading criteria in the hobby. (Note that the first two categories below can also be used to assess the wear on a card's edges.)

Corner with a Slight Touch of Wear: The corner still is sharp, but shows a slight touch of wear. On a dark-bordered card, such wear appears as a white dot.

Fuzzy Corner: The corner still comes to a point, but the point has just begun to fray. A slightly "dinged" corner is considered the same as a fuzzy corner.

Slightly Rounded Corner: The fraying of the corner has increased to the degree at which there remains only a hint of a point. The term *layering* refers to the level at which the individual layers of cardboard start to separate and become evident. A "dinged" corner is considered the same as a slightly rounded corner.

Rounded Corner: The point is completely gone. Some layering is noticeable.

Badly Rounded Corner: The corner is completely round and rough. Severe layering is evident.

Creases

In assessing the condition of a card, a third issue of concern is creasing. The degree of creasing in a card is difficult to illustrate in a drawing or picture. Thus, when providing the specific condition of an expensive card for sale, the seller should note any creases clearly. Creases are categorized on the basis of their severity according to the following scale:

Light Crease: A *light crease* is a crease that is barely noticeable upon close inspection. In fact, when cards are in plastic sheets or holders, a light crease may not be seen at all (until the card is removed from the holder). A light crease on the front of a card is much more serious than a light crease on the card back only.

Medium Crease: A *medium crease* is noticeable when a card is held and studied at arm's length by the naked eye, but does not overly detract from the appearance of the card. It is an obvious crease, but not one that breaks the picture surface of the card.

Heavy Crease: A *heavy crease* is one that has torn or broken through the card's picture surface.

Alterations

Deceptive Trimming: This occurs when someone alters a card in order to (1) shave off edge wear, (2) improve the sharpness of the corners, or (3) improve centering. Obviously, that person's objective is to falsely increase the perceived value of the card to an unsuspecting buyer. The shrinkage usually is evident only if the trimmed card is compared to an adjacent full-sized card or if the trimmed card itself is measured.

Obvious Trimming: *Obvious trimming* is noticeable and unfortunate. It is usually performed by noncollectors who give no thought to the present or future value of their cards.

Deceptively Retouched Borders: This occurs when the borders of a card (especially a card with dark borders) are touched up on the edges and corners with a Magic Marker or crayon in order to make the card appear to be in mint condition.

The condition of a card will vary based on all of these factors, and cards in better condition will always demand higher prices on the secondary, or collectors', market. Based on these factors, some collectors will attempt to determine for themselves the condition—and therefore the value—of a card, and will use that determination to decide how much they are willing to pay for the card. Other collectors will only purchase cards that have been professionally "graded," based on terms that will be discussed at greater length in chapter 3. Either way, the smart collector should always be careful to check the condition of a card carefully before purchasing—it can be the difference between a great deal and a terrible one.

3

LEARN THE LINGO

If you're going to be a sports card expert, you've got to know the language. After all, you don't want to walk into your local hobby shop or attend a sports card show not having a clue about what anyone is saying. This chapter presents a few key terms that will have you talking—and listening—like an expert in no time.

Book Value (HI book, LO book): You will often hear collectors and dealers refer to a card's book value. Sports card price guides, such as *Beckett Baseball*, *Tuff Stuff*, and *Card Trade*, track the secondary market values of cards. The prices of the cards are listed in the publications, which are essential tools for any expert. Most price guides include a HI and LO price listing. This reflects the highest and lowest prices at which a card is currently trading.

Common: A less-than-flattering term for a card that is considered virtually worthless by most collectors. The good thing about collecting, though, is that one collector's common can be another's superstar.

Double Print: An outdated term, *double print* refers to those cards that are printed with more frequency than other cards in a set. Since cards are printed on large 100- or 110-card sheets, or *forms*, a double print occurs when one player's card appears twice on a sheet.

Dupe: Short for *duplicate,* this term refers to a card that is the same as one you already possess. Dupes are also known as *extras.*

Error Cards: The most common errors on cards include misspellings, incorrect birth dates, printing mistakes, and erroneous statistics. Such errors are more common with older cards. The only time an error adds value to a card is if the company stops the presses and creates a corrected version of the card. However, this rarely happens anymore because of the expense involved, thereby ensuring that error cards rarely have additional value. Error cards do sometimes appear, however, and collectors sometimes put a premium on certain examples of such cards. Note that some sports card price guides denote error cards using the abbreviations ERR, COR (for *corrected cards,* which are versions of error cards that were fixed by the manufacturer), and UER (for uncorrected error cards, which are error cards not corrected by the manufacturer).

Grading Terms: *Graded cards* are cards that have been submitted to an independent service for certification of condition and preservation within a sealed holder. Professional grading services are growing in popularity, because a card's grade is a major determinant of its secondary market value. Although not all graded cards earn a premium on the secondary market, those rare cards that receive high grades often sell for prices significantly above book values for *raw,* or ungraded, cards. That's because cards in Gem Mint or Pristine condition are quite scarce, and therefore quite desirable. The demand for these cards exceeds the supply, which leads to higher prices. The top three grading companies are Beckett Grading Services (BGS), Professional Sports Authenticator (PSA), and Sportscard Guaranty, LLC

(SGC). For more information on these companies, see the resource guide in part 3. The terms most collectors use when referring to grading levels and the condition of cards are as follows:

A graded 1952 Topps Mickey Mantle card

Mint (Mt): Denotes a card with no flaws or wear. A *Mint* card has four perfect corners, 60/40 or better centering from top to bottom and from left to right, original gloss, smooth edges, and original color borders. A *Mint* card does not have print spots, color imperfections, or focus imperfections.

Near Mint–Mint (NrMt–Mt): Denotes a card with one minor flaw. Any one of the following flaws would lower the grade of a *Mint* card to *Near Mint–Mint*: one corner with a slight touch of wear, barely noticeable print spots, or color or focus imperfections. A Near Mint–Mint card must have 60/40 or better centering in both directions, original gloss, smooth edges, and original color borders.

Near Mint (NrMt): Denotes a card with one minor flaw. Any one of the following flaws would lower the grade of a *Mint* card to *Near Mint*: one fuzzy corner or two to four corners with slight touches of wear, 70/30 to 60/40 centering, slightly rough edges, minor print spots, or color or focus imperfections. A *Near Mint* card must have original gloss and original color borders.

Excellent-Mint (ExMt): Denotes a card with two or three fuzzy—but not rounded—corners and centering no worse than 80/20. An *Excellent-Mint* card may have no more than two of the following flaws: slightly rough edges, very slightly discolored borders, minor print spots, or color or focus imperfections. The card must have original gloss.

Excellent (Ex): Denotes a card with four fuzzy—but definitely not rounded—corners and centering no worse than 80/20. The card may have a small amount of original gloss lost, rough edges, slightly discolored borders, and minor print spots, or color or focus imperfections.

Very Good (Vg): Denotes a card that has been handled but not abused: slightly rounded corners with slight layering, slight notching on edges, a significant amount of gloss lost from the surface but no scuffing, and moderate discoloration of borders. The card may have a few light creases.

Good (G), Fair (F), or **Poor (P):** These terms denote well-worn, mishandled, or abused cards: badly rounded and layered corners, scuffing, most or all of the original gloss missing, seriously discolored borders, moderate or heavy creases, and one or more serious flaws. The grading of a card as *Good, Fair,* or *Poor* depends on the severity of wear and flaws. A *Good* card is acceptable to many collectors; Fair and Poor cards generally are used only as fillers.

The most widely used grades are defined above. Obviously, many cards will not fit perfectly into one of these categories. Therefore, collectors often designate categories between the major grades, known as *in-between grades,* such as *Good to Very Good* (G–Vg), *Very Good to Excellent* (Vg–Ex), and *Excellent-Mint* to *Near Mint* (ExMt–NrMt).

Hits: This is not an official term by any means, but many collectors have picked it up over the past few years. It is loosely used to refer to the "good" cards a collector gets from a box. For example, if a collector gets four good cards from a box, then that box is said to have four *hits.*

Hot Box or Hot Pack: Refers to boxes or packs that intentionally deliver more inserts or hits than advertised or expected. If, for example, you're supposed to get only four inserts in a box and you get ten, then you've opened a *hot box.*

Insert Card: Also commonly referred to as a *chase card,* an *insert card* is any card that comes in a pack that is not part of the main set. Traditionally, insert cards are printed in smaller quantities than regular cards, and therefore tend to sell for higher prices. Today, inserts feature various pieces of memorabilia, autographs, and multiple players.

Memorabilia Card: *Memorabilia cards* feature a small piece of game-worn or game-used memorabilia—such as a swatch of a player's jersey or a splinter of a player's bat—affixed to the card. These cards created a frenzy when they first appeared on the market in 1996 and are still incredibly popular with collectors.

One-of-One: This term is used to describe a card that is one of a kind—in other words, the card company produced just one. Typically, these cards will be numbered on the back as "1/1." A one-of-one may also be referred to in the marketplace as a *masterpiece,* a nod to Fleer, which introduced the industry's first one-of-ones in an insert set called "Masterpiece."

Parallel: A *parallel* is a special insert card that features the same photo and design elements as a regular card, but adds distinguishing features such as background color, die-cutting, foil elements, or serial numbering. Parallels typically are scarcer than regular cards, and therefore are more expensive. To determine the value of a parallel card, look for the multipliers that are listed under the title of the appropriate set.

Pull: To take a card from a pack or box, or the term for any card that is so taken. For example: "I pulled a Roger Clemens autograph." "Wow, nice pull!"

Rookie Card: A *Rookie Card* is the regular-issue card from a major card company on which a player makes his first appearance. For purposes of this definition, major card companies include Donruss Playoff, Fleer, Pacific, Topps, and Upper Deck. In many cases, a player appears on a card before he ever plays in the major leagues. In hobby publications and price guides, you will often see "Rookie Card" abbreviated as "RC."

Serial Number: Many Rookie Cards, inserts, parallels, and (in some cases) base cards are sequentially numbered. Such numbering almost always takes the form of a stamp on the back or front of the card. For example, if a card is numbered "10/300" on the back, this means that the card is the tenth out of 300 produced. Serial numbering can add to the rarity and exclusivity of a card. Often collectors will say that a certain card is "numbered to" a particular quantity. Some cards are considered more valuable if they possess a special or unique number, such as the player's jersey number, or if the card is the first one produced (i.e., 1/300).

Short Print: A company may intentionally choose to print fewer copies of certain cards than others in the set. This is done to create additional demand for these singles, and to increase the challenge for those building a particular set. You will often see and hear this term abbreviated as "SP."

Singles: This is a term used in the buying and selling of cards. It refers to individual cards as opposed to multiple cards, packs, or boxes of cards. Singles often appear as a separate category on many online sites such as eBay, Beckett.com, and Amazon.com.

Slabbed: Any card that has been professionally graded and encased in a thick plastic case (known as a *slab*) is said to be *slabbed*.

Subset: Unlike parallel or insert cards, *subset cards* are part of a main base set. Subsets are typically found near the end of base sets and are numbered with the base cards. These cards have different designs and features, such as autographs, pieces of memorabilia, or common themes and characteristics such as short-printed rookies or unique artwork.

Swatch: The majority of sports card products feature cards with pieces of game-worn or game-used memorabilia, including jerseys, bats, balls, shoes, etc. These pieces of memorabilia are called *swatches*. A *prime swatch* is one that includes multiple colors and is usually taken from the team logos, nameplates, patches, or numbers of a player's jersey.

XRC: Short for "extended Rookie Card," this term refers to an early card from a player that appears in a nontraditional set. Some card sets are issued in an uncommon way—for example, through the mail only—while others might be printed through a limited license. For a card to be a true RC (and not an XRC), it must be issued in a fully licensed, mainstream set.

4

BUYING AND SELLING CARDS

With so many products from which to choose, many new collectors simply do not know what to buy, even if they know the players and teams they want to collect. Whatever your area of interest, base your purchases on what you would like to own—not on a card's potential value. If you're looking for an investment vehicle, you face the chance of disappointment. But if you're buying something you like, price fluctuations just won't matter to you. The number one rule in buying and collecting cards is to have fun. After all, there's nothing like opening a pack and pulling your favorite rookie or a memorabilia card featuring a baseball legend.

But to get started, you've got to know where to buy. Thousands of places around the country sell baseball cards, including sports card and memorabilia stores, grocery stores, department stores, and convenience stores. You can also purchase cards at trading card shows or on the Internet. A sports card store is the best place for a new collector to start. It's also the best place to see a large variety of cards and get answers to your collecting questions. There are two easy ways to find your local card shop: by using Major League Baseball dealer locator services (1-877-CARD-MLB, or online at *www.mlb.com*), or by using the card companies' Web sites, which feature search functions.

Currently, Major League Baseball and its players *license* (i.e., contractually allow) two companies—Topps and Upper Deck—to produce trading cards of major-league players and distribute them on a national basis. In football, the NFL and its players license three companies (Topps, Upper Deck, and Donruss/Playoff) to produce and distribute cards, and another company, Press Pass, is licensed by the NFL players alone. Hockey has a single licensee, Upper Deck. Press Pass makes NASCAR trading cards, and Upper Deck makes golf cards using licenses from the PGA and LPGA.

There are many ways to buy and collect cards. At hobby shops, you can buy boxes, packs, or single cards. Each option has its advantages; thus, the choice of how to buy cards will greatly depend on your budget and how much you like a certain product. Keep in mind that every product offers something different.

Buying boxes will give you the best chance of acquiring better cards. Box prices can range anywhere from $60 to a few hundred dollars. Boxes are broken down into packs, and the typical box will include around twenty packs. Your local card dealer should be able to tell you the differences between boxes. Some boxes offer more Rookie Cards, and others deliver more memorabilia and autographed cards. With some boxes, you're more likely to get a high percentage of base cards, which is good for set collectors.

Buying individual packs is of course cheaper than buying boxes. However, your chances of pulling top cards are smaller if you buy a pack than if you buy a box. Depending on the product, packs can contain anywhere from three to ten cards. Again, prices will depend on the individual product.

Hobby Shops vs the Internet

Internet auction and store sites, such as eBay and Beckett.com, have greatly influenced the hobby since the late 1990s. The Internet makes a huge selection available to collectors. Boxes, single cards, autographs; you name it, you can find it online. Moreover, since the law of supply and demand still governs this aspect of the hobby, an overabundance of certain cards can translate to lower prices, which means you can often find cheaper prices online.

However, buying online does have obvious disadvantages. One problem you may encounter is the difficulty of determining the condition of cards you want to buy. Online sellers often display pictures of the cards for sale, but looking at pictures is not an ideal way to scrutinize a card's condition. Another problem is seller credibility. Unless you know the seller from whom you are buying, an online transaction will always involve at least some risk. Most Internet trading sites use some type of feedback system to rate their members. This allows for positive or negative comments to be posted about virtually every online transaction, whether a sale or a purchase. In turn, such comments can give you some insight into whether a buyer or seller is trustworthy.

In addition to being mindful of feedback ratings, buying professionally graded and "slabbed" cards is another way to ensure that cards you buy online will be worth the money. Hobby shops, although their selection may lack the breadth offered by the Internet, are still the best options when it comes to security. Having the physical cards in front of you gives you a closer, more detailed look at the cards you want to buy. A face-to-face transaction can give you a better sense of a card's condition, and may even allow you to score some good bargains and trades with the shop owners. And don't ever be afraid to bargain with shop owners. Some are easier to work with than others, but they aren't called "dealers" for nothing.

Card Shows and Conventions

The popularity of Internet trading, with the freedom it grants collectors to buy and sell trading cards all over the world from the comfort of their own homes, has slightly diminished the role of once-booming national and regional card shows. Still, there's no denying that these gatherings—although smaller in size and frequency than in days past—retain a permanent place in the hobby as hubs of collecting activity. For collectors, there remains an overwhelming allure in gathering with other like-minded, sports-loving collectors to marvel at the sheer quality and abundance of sports collectibles and memorabilia available on the market—often museum-quality stuff that you just don't get to see at your local card shop. Before the Internet, larger card conventions and smaller card shows were seemingly as vital to the collecting hobby as the cards themselves. Conventions and shows were where you went to finish your sets, to buy the newest—and oldest—products on the market, and to trade what you didn't want for the things you did; they were likely your best and final hope for finding that one card that had eluded you.

Attending conventions and shows is a wonderful and usually inexpensive way to immerse yourself in collecting culture—to soak up the atmosphere and hone your trading and bartering skills with dealers who set up tables to sell their wares. Shows also provide a bargain hunter's dream; with so much competition in one room, collectors almost always get the best deals on cards or boxes of cards. Some of the most popular attractions at shows today are insert-card "bargain bins": boxes filled with relatively inexpensive game-used memorabilia, certified autographs, and other insert cards that are typically priced to sell at well below book value. If you're planning to attend a show or convention for the first time, or for the first time in a long time, be prepared. Know beforehand what you're looking for and create a list for yourself that details by set, player, and card number the specific cards you're looking to acquire. Also, conduct preliminary research on the show itself to find out pertinent details such as admission and parking costs, as well as who might be signing autographs at the show, and on which days.

Once inside the show, it's a smart practice to canvass the entire show floor to see what's available before making any purchases. The last thing you want to do is buy the first card on your list that you see, only to find the same card for a much lower price at a table nearby. Also, remember that the best time to buy is near closing time on any show day, but especially on the last day, when most dealers would much rather sell their inventory than pack it up and lug it home. Not surprisingly, most of the bigger, more successful conventions are held in cities with traditionally strong collector bases such as New York, Los Angeles, Chicago, and Cleveland. Having said that, there's nothing quite like taking in a small show at, say, a high school gymnasium to benefit the local booster club. Either way—huge convention or minuscule show— you owe it to yourself to take in at least one or two shows a year if at all possible. There's probably no better way to get a crash course in all that the trading card hobby is, was, and will be.

The best way to familiarize yourself with shows or conventions in your area is to peruse the sections of industry magazines that publish convention calendars. In addition, many show promoters advertise upcoming events in the sports sections of local newspapers and on local radio stations. Finally, you can gather useful information on upcoming shows, as well as read reviews from collectors who have attended, on any number of card industry message boards such as *www.beckett.com* and *www.traderretreat.com*.

The National Sports Collectors Convention
The granddaddy of all sports cards conventions, the National Sports Collectors Convention remains the largest show on the circuit. Each year it draws between 30,000 and 60,000 attendees, depending on the show's location and the climate of the sports card industry during the year. The National, as it's known by industry veterans, is held every summer and rotates among venues, having recently made

Don Williams of Upper Deck talks with a collector at the 2005 National Sports Collectors Convention.

stops in Cleveland (2004 and 2001), Atlantic City (2003), and Chicago (2002). The National celebrated its twenty-fifth anniversary in 2004 and, after all these years, is still something of a mecca for sports card collectors, who flock from all over the country to experience the full scope of the collectibles industry. Everybody who's anybody in the trading card industry sets up shop at the National: card manufacturers, card grading services, sports collectibles publishers, online trading companies, auction houses, trading card distributors, and 200 to 300 sports collectibles and memorabilia dealers, considered by many to be the lifeblood of the industry. Each year the National also features a stunningly impressive autograph lineup, drawing Hall of Famers and superstars from the four major sports, as well as other popular entertainers. Add it all up and you've got quite an impressive assemblage of industry clout, not to mention a nice overall reflection of industry activity for the year. And although, thanks to the Internet, it's not nearly as grand or as necessary as it once was, the National remains a viable and widely embraced institution in the trading card hobby.

Other Conventions

In the 21st century, the hobby's card show circuit is composed largely of smaller regional shows put together by local promoters. A few larger shows also take place on an annual basis, including Krause Publications' SportsFest (usually in June) and the popular *Chicago Sun-Times* shows that are typically conducted twice each year (in the spring and fall). Tri-Star Productions, a successful show-promotion company that also holds exclusive autograph agreements with many of the top athletes in sports, conducts a string of well-attended card shows throughout the year. For more information on Tri-Star's show schedule, visit the company's Web site at *www.tristarproductions.com*. If you're having a difficult time locating a show in your area, try doing a search for "card shows" on an Internet search engine such as Google (*www.google.com*).

The League Shows

Each of the four major sports leagues conducts some manner of trading card show in conjunction with its crown-jewel event (for Major League Baseball, the NBA, and the NHL, these shows occur during the respective all-star game celebrations; for the NFL, the show occurs during the Super Bowl). Although they're not typically intense collector-based shows on par with the National, the league shows provide wonderful opportunities for card manufacturers and dealers to expose their industry to much larger, fan-based audiences. Each of these shows, including Major League Baseball's All-Star FanFest, draws huge numbers of sports fans from around the country. And though card shows constitute only a small part of these massive, league-themed festivals, the sheer amount of traffic in the card show areas invariably provides wonderful exposure for the collectibles industry. Since the clientele at these events is so different from the clientele at other conventions—largely non-collecting sports fans as opposed to hard-core collectors—the types of cards and collectibles for sale is vastly different, too. Lower-priced card packs and inexpensive memorabilia (such as mini-helmets, pennants, bobbleheads, and the like) tend to fare very well at these events.

From a trading card perspective, some of the most successful elements of league shows are *wrapper redemption programs* conducted by various card manufacturers in conjunction with the leagues. Pursuant to these programs, each licensed card maker (in baseball, that's Topps and Upper Deck) produces special cards available exclusively at the show through a wrapper exchange. Typically, each manufacturer will produce four special cards, usually depicting locally popular players, creating an eight-card set. In order to obtain those cards, show-goers must open a specified number of each manufacturer's current baseball packs and exchange the wrappers for the special cards. In a nod to the increasing popularity of game-worn memorabilia cards, Major League Baseball has incorporated special versions of such cards into its wrapper redemption program in recent years. Aside from the wrapper redemption programs, card manufacturers also use league shows to introduce themselves to potential new customers through promotions and giveaways.

Conferences

There is but one true conference conducted by the heavyweights of the card collecting industry, and it occurs in Hawaii, of all places, every February. Set in serene surroundings, the aptly named Hawaii Trade Conference (formerly the Kit Young Trade Conference before collectibles publisher Krause Publications took over the event a few years ago) is a one-week powwow at which the industry's key players can reflect on the previous year, the future, and the overriding issues affecting the collectibles industry.

Every conceivable player in the industry converges on Hawaii for this annual conference: collectibles representatives and licensing bigwigs from all the sports leagues, executives from every card manufacturer and collectibles company, industry media, the biggest trading card distributors (whose job it is to get the cards from the companies to the dealers), and dealers. And although the event includes its fair share of social functions such as receptions and evening parties, the conference is also tremendously productive in terms of facilitating interaction between people at every level of the sports card food chain. Perhaps the Hawaii Trade Conference's greatest strength is providing store owners a direct audience with card company representatives, and vice versa. Expert panel discussions and seminars—on topics ranging from marketing to merchandising to customer service—consume most days of the conference, and most convention-goers take full advantage of their proximity to key players by scheduling myriad informal meetings.

For card manufacturers, the Hawaii Trade Conference is an invaluable opportunity to preview releases for the coming year and to exchange meaningful dialogue with the dealers and distributors who sell their trading card products throughout the year. Most manufacturers distribute scarce and usually valuable special collectibles to the 300 or so people in attendance every year, and receive vital feedback—both good and bad—that helps them make meaningful business decisions in the future. The Hawaii Trade Conference celebrated its twentieth anniversary in 2005.

What's It Worth? A Quick Look at Price Guides

Over the years, the trading card industry has been previewed, probed, reviewed, revered, tracked, teased, chronicled, and critiqued by myriad monthly and annual publications, the vast majority of which have boasted woefully short life spans. But in spite of all those here-today-gone-tomorrow publications, two companies, Beckett Media and Krause Publications, have stood the test of time. Today, those companies function as something like the official chroniclers of the sports collecting hobby, and as the chief avenues for card makers and collectibles producers to deliver their respective messages.

Here's a brief look at each:

Beckett Media

Started in 1984 by Dr. James Beckett, Beckett Media is known for its comprehensive, accurate price guides and its informative editorial content. Beckett Media boasts five nationally distributed monthly magazines devoted exclusively to coverage of sports cards and collectibles: *Beckett Baseball, Beckett Bas-*

ketball, Beckett Football, Beckett Hockey, and *Beckett Racing.* In addition, Beckett produces two in-depth bimonthly publications devoted to baseball and racing, and three quarterly publications dedicated to football, basketball, and hockey.

At the height of its pre-Internet popularity, Beckett was arguably the most powerful entity in the hobby because its in-demand price guides were the first to reflect the secondary market value for every trading card produced. Although Beckett always has contended that its price guides are *guides* and nothing more, this position is a hard sell for the vast majority of buyers and sellers who have come to rely heavily on its invaluable pricing data.

Using its popular Web site (*www.beckett.com*), Beckett has aggressively diversified, expanding beyond magazines to become something of a one-stop shop for collectors. (For more information about the services offered by Beckett, see the "Online Resources" section in part 3 of this book.) For each major sport, Beckett also produces a voluminous annual almanac that provides painstaking and exhaustive cataloging, information, and pricing for virtually every trading card ever produced. These almanacs draw from the efforts of Beckett's monthly magazines throughout the year, as well as other in-house resources and a far-reaching network of regional correspondents who provide often hard-to-find details on "oddball" releases from the last one hundred years.

Krause Publications

With publishing roots dating to 1952, Krause Publications stands as the industry's most venerable media representative. Today Krause maintains three successful titles devoted to sports collectibles, with each geared to a largely different audience.

- *Tuff Stuff,* a monthly price guide and information magazine, is likely Krause's most visible title. Directed at newer collectors, *Tuff Stuff* covers modern cards and memorabilia. Because it covers all four major sports as well as the autograph and collectible-figures segments of the industry, *Tuff Stuff* is able to provide the most comprehensive card pricing and market information available.

- *Sports Collectors Digest* is a weekly oversized tabloid publication and Krause's most mature title. Devoted to an older, more serious collecting audience, it features extensive coverage of the vintage market and the memorabilia auction scene.

- *Krause's Card Trade* is a monthly trade publication that provides information on market activity from dealers, distributors, and other people on the front lines of the industry. It also features useful business tips from the industry's most successful dealers and distributors in regards to promotions, customer service, merchandising, and the like.

Krause also produces a family of exhaustive annual catalogs. The size of phone books, these oversize volumes provide comprehensive pricing and history dating as far back as the late 1800s. For more information on Krause's family of sports collectibles publications, visit *www.collect.com.*

Other Publications

Although lacking the size and scope of Beckett's and Krause's publications, a handful of fringe hobby magazines also delivers timely information to the insatiable collecting audience.

Trajan Publications produces *Canadian Sports Collector,* which, as its name suggests, caters to collectors north of the border. This monthly publication provides extensive coverage of the hockey collectibles market, and perhaps the industry's only coverage of Canadian Football League cards and collectibles. Despite a focus on collectibles devoted to the key Canadian sports, *Canadian Sports Collector* also provides pricing and editorial coverage of baseball, American football, and basketball cards. Like its American counterparts, Trajan produces an exhaustive annual catalog dedicated to the proud history of hockey cards. For more information on *Canadian Sports Collector*, visit the magazine's Web site at *www.cscmag.ca*.

5

PROTECTING YOUR COLLECTION

Names to Know

No matter what the value of your collection, it's always a good idea to keep your cards protected. Since different cards have different values, be they monetary or sentimental, various methods and degrees of protection may be appropriate for different cards. The industry leaders in card protection products are

- Ultra-PRO
- Pro-Mold
- Cardboard Gold
- Max Protection

Tools of the Trade

Penny Sleeves: These are ordinary soft plastic sleeves. Many collectors will put their cards in thin *penny sleeves* before putting them in better, more rigid card protectors.

A StorSafe top loader

Otherwise, penny sleeves are for common cards with little value. At best, they protect the cards from minor scratches, dust, and fingerprints. Penny sleeves can be found in packs of 100 for around $1.

Semi-Rigid Holders: *Semi-rigid holders* are thin plastic protectors. Essentially, they are one step up from penny sleeves—although it is a big step. They're longer than most other holders, which can make them difficult to store. These protectors are not as widely used as they once were.

Top Loaders: These protectors are thicker than semi-rigid holders and are smaller, making for easy storage. They are called *top loaders* because the cards are inserted from the top. Top loaders are ideal for protecting lower-end cards. Many collectors choose to put their cards in penny sleeves before they insert them into top loaders, which can be purchased in packs of twenty-five. Some include colored borders and the words "Rookie Card" at the top.

Snap-Tights: These are two-piece plastic holders that snap together to hold the cards. Their thickness can vary. A disadvantage to these holders is that they tend to break apart when they are dropped.

Screwdowns: These are the most popular card protectors. *Screwdowns* feature either one screw or four screws, one at each corner. Like snap-tights, the thickness of these holders will vary. Memorabilia cards, for example, require thicker screwdowns. Many four-screw screwdowns provide better protection, and some feature recessed areas in which to fit the card. This can keep the holder from touching the front of the card, which can be important for autograph cards because it prevents the ink from transferring onto the holder. Thicker screwdowns, such as 1/2-inch and 1-inch sizes, are ideal for vintage cards. They also make for nice displays.

Storage Boxes: *Storage boxes* have come a long way from the days when cards were stored in old shoeboxes, and today's collectors have many options. Storage boxes can be used to store common cards, and some companies produce plastic boxes big enough to store complete sets, depending on the set's size. Some cardboard boxes are even big enough to store up to 5,000 cards.

Binders and Pages: Another option for storing card sets is to use three-ring *binders* with nine-card *pages*. Cards are more viewable when stored in this way, since you can easily flip through the pages. Most binders and pages are sold separately. Ultra-PRO makes binders for different sports. Boxes of 100 nine-card pages can be purchased for around $15.

6

COUNTERFEITS

How Not to Get Ripped Off

Almost anything of value has the potential to be counterfeited. The sports card marketplace is no exception, and fakes have surfaced for many top cards. To the untrained eye, a solid fake can be deceptive enough to change hands multiple times before anyone notices. And now that online purchases have become overwhelmingly common, it is even easier to be taken in by a counterfeit. Today more and more cards are bought sight unseen (often online), with blurry or minuscule scans, or even with *switched scans* (when legitimate cards are pictured but the actual cards received are fakes). Particularly with online transactions, the vast array of counterfeiting possibilities only increases the odds that any given collector may become a victim. Usually, matching a card against a known legitimate card will clearly identify an impostor, but how many collectors carry around a stack of samples? If another sample is unavailable, a common card from the same set will often be just as helpful.

If you receive a card and have doubts as to its legitimacy, it is best to take the card to reputable dealers or collectors to ask their opinions. If you are still not satisfied, or prefer a more definitive answer right away, send the card to a professional grading service. If the card is returned ungraded, be sure to save any paperwork you receive and keep the card in the original holder in which it was returned, in case you choose to pursue legal action.

While it can be difficult to retrieve your money from a seller, it is not impossible. If the seller was an innocent victim as well, he or she may be more willing to work with you. If the seller is the counterfeiter, or is working in conjunction with the counterfeiter, you may be out of luck. Pursue the matter with the site at which the purchase was made, and consider filing fraud charges with the appropriate agencies. In some instances, the card manufacturers themselves have stepped in to pursue those counterfeiting their cards.

When assessing a card's authenticity, consider the following key factors:

Weight

Weight is one of the easiest factors to consider, but the problem is that few collectors have access to a fine digital scale, which is the best equipment for weighing cards. Any scale that weighs to the hundredth of a gram will suffice. The majority of counterfeits weigh either significantly more or less than real cards, as it is impossible to perfectly duplicate the card stock used for an original. Weigh several samples from the real set, as some sets naturally fluctuate greatly. For most sets, any variance of more than a tenth of a gram should raise a red flag. Size is not usually an issue, but a number of fakes will measure too long or too short.

Dot Pattern

When assessing the authenticity of a card, another major area of concern is dot pattern. Anyone who deals in high-end Rookie Cards, vintage material, or

Areas of black text are some of the first giveaways of a counterfeit. On the 1980 Topps Rickey Henderson fake shown above, the letters in Henderson's name are composed of numerous dots, as opposed to the solid black ink of an original. On the fake, a green and white dot pattern constitutes the background of Henderson's "A's" logo; on a real issue, the green background is solid. Note the broken circle surrounding the © logo on the Henderson counterfeit's back.

other high-ticket items should invest in a quality loupe. The choices are numerous, but we suggest a 16X doublet. Such loupes are small, but have a reasonably large field of vision, and cost just a third of what triplet loupes cost. Using this type of loupe, examine any of a card's printing areas, but primarily the black inked portions and the text. On a genuine sample, search for areas that are printed in solid ink; on a counterfeit card, search for small print dots. Fake cards are usually rescreened, which results in a blurry appearance. Copying a card on a photocopier will typically leave this kind of pattern; the counterfeiting process uses small dots to create the card. Some counterfeiters will rescreen the entire card, while others do a more professional job of rescreening only the photo, and rebuilding the other design elements from scratch.

Photo Sharpness and Feel

While examining a card's weight and dot pattern are the major means of identifying most counterfeits, there are a handful of other tricks. Counterfeit photos are usually blurred or faded, or simply show less contrast. Color ink may appear far brighter than usual or, on the opposite end of the spectrum, may appear far too dull. Minute areas of text typically blur together into an unreadable mess. The counterfeit card may display a different "feel"—either too thick or thin, too cleanly or roughly cut, or even slightly "rubbery."

Rules of Thumb

It is difficult to create a simple catch-all rule for weeding out counterfeits. As each new counterfeiting method is discovered, a new one pops up soon after. A poorly faked card might be recounterfeited later, removing the elements that easily marked it as an imitation. As always, the best rule is to be very careful, especially if a deal seems too good to be true, or if you are dealing with any high-end cards. However, even low-dollar cards have been counterfeited over the years. If in doubt, find another sample of the same card with which to compare it, but if the same card is not available, a common card from the same set will often be just as helpful. Also, don't be afraid to ask questions or seek advice from a hobby dealer or advanced collector.

Part 2

THE HISTORY OF SPORTS CARDS

To truly appreciate where the hobby of sports card collecting is today, it's necessary to understand where it has been. Here is an exhaustive look at the varied, proud histories of America's four favorite collecting sports—from their beginnings to the present day.

7

THE HISTORY OF BASEBALL CARDS

Today's version of the baseball card, with its colorful and often high-tech front and back, is a far cry from its earliest predecessors. The issue remains cloudy as to which was the very first baseball card ever produced, but the institution of baseball cards dates from the latter half of the 19th century. Early issues, generally printed on heavy cardboard, were of poor quality, with photographs, drawings, and printing falling far short of today's standards.

Goodwin & Co. of New York, makers of Gypsy Queen, Old Judge, and other cigarette brands, is considered by many to be the first issuer of baseball and other sports cards. Its issues, predominantly sized 1-1/2 x 2-1/2 inches, generally consisted of photographs of baseball players, boxers, wrestlers, and other subjects mounted on stiff cardboard. More than 2,000 different photos of baseball players alone have been identified. These *Old Judges,* a collective name commonly used for the Goodwin & Co. cards, were issued from 1886 to 1890 and are treasured parts of many collections today.

By 1895, the American Tobacco Company began to dominate its competition. No longer needing the promotional boost provided by cards, they discontinued card inserts in their cigarette packages (which were actually slide boxes in those days), marking the end of the first era of baseball cards. Thus, at the dawn of the 20th century, few baseball cards were being issued. But once again it was the cigarette companies—particularly the American Tobacco Company, followed to a lesser extent by candy and gum makers—that revived the practice of including baseball cards with their products. The bulk of these cards, identified in J.R. Burdick's *The American Card Catalog* as *T* or *E cards* (for 20th-century "Tobacco" or "Early Candy and Gum" issues, respectively), were released from 1909 to 1915.

This romantic and popular era of baseball card collecting produced many desirable items. The most outstanding is the fabled T206 Honus Wagner card, considered the holy grail of baseball cards and the most valuable trading card in the world. One of the few Wagners remaining in existence sold for more than $1.2 million in a 2000 eBay auction. As the rumor goes, Wagner disapproved of his cards being associated with a tobacco product and had them removed from production—but not before a precious few of them made their way into circulation. Another theory that has gained acceptance in recent years suggests that Wagner was dissatisfied with the compensation being offered for the use of his image. At any rate, fewer than 100 Wagner cards are known to exist. Other perennial favorites from that era are the T206 Eddie Plank card and the T206 Sherry Magee error card. The former was once the second most valuable card in the world, and only recently relinquished that position to a more distinctive and aesthetically pleasing Napoleon Lajoie card from the 1933–34 Goudey Gum series. The Magee card misspells the player's name as "Magie" and is the world's most famous and most valuable blooper card.

While the American Tobacco Company dominated the field of baseball cards, several other tobacco companies—as well as clothing manufacturers, newspapers and periodicals, game makers, and other companies whose identities were lost to time—also issued cards during this period. The Collins-McCarthy Candy Company, makers of Zeenuts Pacific Coast League baseball cards, issued cards yearly from 1911 to 1938. Its record for continuous annual card production has been exceeded only by Topps. The era of the tobacco issues closed with the onset of World War I, with the exception of the Red Man chewing tobacco sets produced from 1952 to 1955.

1909 T206
Honus Wagner

The next flurry of card issues occurred during the roaring and prosperous 1920s, the era of the E card. The caramel companies (National Caramel, American Caramel, York Caramel) were the leading distributors of these E cards. In addition, the *strip card,* a continuous strip composed of several cards divided by dotted lines or other sectioning features, flourished during this time. While these E cards and strip cards generally are considered less imaginative than T cards or recent candy and gum issues, they are still pursued by many advanced collectors because of the key players they feature, such as Babe Ruth, Ty Cobb, and "Shoeless" Joe Jackson.

Another significant event of the 1920s was the introduction of the *arcade card.* Taking its designation from its issuer, the Exhibit Supply Company of Chicago, the arcade card is usually known as the *Exhibit card.* Once a trademark of penny arcades, amusement parks, and county fairs across the country, Exhibit machines dispensed postcard-size photos on thick stock for one penny. These picture cards bore likenesses of a favorite cowboy, actor, actress, or baseball player. Though it did not produce continuously, Exhibit Supply and its associated companies produced baseball cards during a longer time span than any other manufacturer. Its first cards appeared in 1921, and its last issue came in 1966. In 1979, the Exhibit Supply Company was bought and somewhat revived by a collector/dealer who has since reprinted Exhibit photos from the past.

If the T card period from 1909 to 1915 can be designated the "golden age" of baseball card collecting, then perhaps the "silver age" commenced with the introduction of the Big League Gum series of 239 cards in 1933 (a 240th card was added in 1934). These cards were the forerunners of today's baseball gum cards, and the Goudey Gum Company of Boston is responsible for their success. This era spanned the period from the Depression days of 1933 to America's formal involvement in World War II in 1941. Goudey's attractive designs, with full-color line drawings on thick card stock, greatly influenced other cards being issued at that time. As a result, the most attractive and popular vintage cards in history were produced during this period. The 1933 Goudey Big League Gum series also owes its popularity to the more than forty Hall of Fame players featured in the set, which included four cards of Babe Ruth and two of Lou Gehrig.

Goudey's reign continued in 1934, when it issued a ninety-six-card set in color, together with the single remaining card from the 1933 series, #106, the Napoleon Lajoie card. In addition to Goudey, several other bubble gum manufacturers issued baseball cards during this era. DeLong Gum Company issued an extremely attractive set in 1933. National Chicle Company's 192-card Batter-Up series of 1934–1936 became the largest die-cut set in card history. In addition, that company offered the popular Diamond Stars series during the same period. Other popular sets included the Tattoo Orbit set of sixty color cards issued in 1933 and Gum Products' seventy-five-card Double Play set, featuring sepia depictions of two players per card.

Gum Inc., which later became Bowman Gum, replaced Goudey Gum in 1939 as the leading baseball card producer. In 1939 and 1940 it issued two important sets of black-and-white cards. In 1939, its Play Ball America set consisted of 162 cards. The larger, 240-card Play Ball set of 1940 is still considered by many to be the most attractive set of black-and-white cards ever produced. Gum Inc. introduced its only color set in 1941, consisting of seventy-two cards and titled Play Ball Sports Hall of Fame. Many of these cards were colored repeats of poses from the black-and-white 1940 series.

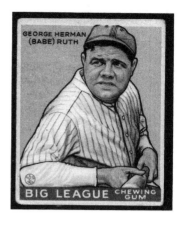

1933 Goudey
Babe Ruth
#181

In addition to regular gum cards, many manufacturers distributed premium issues during the 1930s. These premiums were printed on paper or photographic stock rather than card stock. They were much larger than regular cards and were sold for a penny across the counter with gum (which was packaged separately from the premium). They were often acquired at the store or through the mail in exchange for the wrappers of previously purchased gum cards, like proof-of-purchase box-top premiums today. The gum premiums are more scarce than the card issues of the 1930s, and in most cases they are not imprinted with the manufacturer's name.

World War II brought an end to this popular era of card collecting when paper and rubber shortages curtailed the production of bubble gum baseball cards. But they were revived in 1948 by the Bowman Gum Company, the direct descendant of Gum Inc. This marked the beginning of the modern era of card collecting.

In 1948, Bowman Gum released a forty-eight-card black-and-white set, issued in one-cent packs containing one card and one piece of gum each. That same year, the Leaf Gum Company also issued a set of cards. Although rather poor in quality, these cards were printed in color. A squabble over the rights to use players' pictures developed between Bowman and Leaf. Eventually Leaf dropped out of the card market, but not before it had left a lasting mark on the hobby by issuing some of the rarest cards now in existence. Leaf's baseball card series of 1948–49 contained ninety-eight cards, *skip-numbered* to #168 (not all numbers were printed). Of these ninety-eight cards, forty-nine are relatively plentiful; the other forty-nine, however, are rare and quite valuable.

Bowman continued its production of cards in 1949 with a color series of 240 cards. Because it contains many scarce "high numbers," this series remains the most difficult Bowman regular issue to complete. Although the set was printed in color and commands great interest due to its scarcity, it is considered aesthetically inferior to the Goudey and National Chicle issues of the 1930s. In 1950 (the one year in which Bowman enjoyed a monopoly on the baseball card market), the company began producing a string of top-quality cards that continued until its demise in 1955.

The year 1951 marked the beginning of the most competitive and perhaps the highest-quality period of baseball card production. In that year, Topps Chewing Gum Company of Brooklyn entered the market. The 1951 Topps cards were unattractive, and paled in comparison to the 1951 Bowman issues. But they were successful, and Topps has continued to produce cards ever since.

Topps issued a larger and more attractive card set in 1952. This larger size became standard for the next five years. (Bowman followed with larger-size baseball cards in 1953.) Like the 1933 Goudey series and the T206 white-border series, this 1952 Topps set has become the classic set of its era. The 407-card set is a collector's dream of scarcities, rarities, errors, and variations. It also contains the first Topps issues of Mickey Mantle and Willie Mays.

As with Bowman and Leaf in the late 1940s, competition over player rights arose between Bowman and

Topps, and court battles ensued. The market split due to stiff competition, and Topps bought out Bowman in January 1956. (Topps resurrected the Bowman brand in 1989.) From then until 1980, Topps remained essentially unchallenged as the primary producer of baseball cards. As a result, the story of major baseball card sets from 1956 through 1980 is by and large the story of Topps. Notable exceptions include the small sets produced by Fleer Gum in 1959, 1960, 1961, and 1963, and the Kellogg's Cereal and Hostess Cakes baseball cards issued to promote those companies' products. A court decision in 1980 paved the way for two other large gum companies to enter (or, in Fleer's case, reenter) the baseball card arena. Fleer, which had last made photo cards in 1963, and the Donruss Company (then a division of General Mills) secured rights to produce baseball cards of current players, thus breaking Topps's monopoly.

Each company issued major card sets in 1981 with bubble gum products. Then a higher court decision in that year overturned the lower court ruling against Topps. It appeared that Topps had regained its sole position as a producer of baseball cards. Undaunted by the ruling, Fleer and Donruss continued to issue cards in 1982, but without bubble gum or any other edible product. Fleer issued new baseball cards with team logo stickers, while Donruss issued its cards with pieces of a baseball jigsaw puzzle.

Since 1981, these three major baseball card producers—Topps, Fleer, and Donruss—have all thrived, sharing relatively equal recognition. Each has steadily increased its involvement in terms of numbers of issues per year. To the delight of collectors, the resulting competition has generated novel, and in some cases exceptional, issues of current Major League Baseball players. Collectors also eagerly accepted the debut efforts of Score (1988) and Upper Deck (1989), and the five card-producing companies embarked on quite a wild ride through the 1990s. Upper Deck's successful entry into the market turned out to be extremely important. The company's card stock, photography, packaging, and marketing gave baseball cards a new

Ken Griffey Jr.

1989 Upper
Deck Ken
Griffey Jr. RC

standard for quality and began the "premium card" trend that continues today. The second premium baseball card set to be issued was the 1990 Leaf set, named for and issued by the parent company of Donruss.

To gauge the significance of the premium-card trend, one need only note that two of the most valuable post-1986 regular-issue cards in the hobby are the 1989 Upper Deck Ken Griffey Jr. and 1990 Leaf Sammy Sosa Rookie Cards. Leaf's impressive debut in 1990 was followed by those of Studio, Ultra, and Stadium Club in 1991. Of those, the Topps-owned Stadium Club, with its dramatic borderless-photo and uncoated card fronts, made the biggest impact. In 1992, Bowman and Pinnacle joined the premium fray. In 1992, Donruss and Fleer abandoned the traditional 50-cent pack market and instead produced premium sets comparable to (and presumably designed to compete against) Upper Deck's set. Those moves, combined with the almost instantaneous spread of premium cards to other major-team sports cards markets, served as strong indicators that premium cards were here to stay. In 1993, Fleer, Topps, and Upper Deck produced the first "super premium" cards with Flair, Finest, and SP, respectively. The success of all three products was an indication that the baseball card market was headed toward even higher price levels. This indeed turned out to be the case in 1994, with the introduction of Bowman's Best (a Topps hybrid of prospect-oriented Bowman and the super-premium Finest) and Leaf Limited.

Overall, inserts continued to dominate the hobby scene. Specifically, the parallel chase cards introduced in 1992 with Topps Gold became the latest major hobby trend. Topps Gold was followed by 1993 Finest Refractors (at the time the scarcest insert ever produced, and still a landmark set) and the one-per-box Stadium Club First Day Issue. Of course, the biggest on-field news of 1994 was the owner-provoked players' strike that halted the season prematurely. While the baseball card market suffered noticeably from the strike, there was no catastrophic crash as some had feared. However, the strike drastically slowed down a market that was both strong and growing, and contributed to a serious hobby contraction that continues to this day. By 1995, parallel insert sets were commonplace and had taken on a new complexion: The most popular ones were those with announced (or at least suspected) print runs of 500 or less, such as Finest Refractors and Select Artist's Proofs. This trend continued in 1996, with several parallel inserts that were printed in quantities of 250 or less. It could be argued that the high price tags on these extremely limited parallel cards (many exceeded $1,000) were driving many single-player collectors to frustration, and driving others completely out of the hobby. At the same time, average pack prices soared while the average number of cards per pack dropped, making the baseball card hobby increasingly expensive.

On the positive side, two important and trendsetting releases in 1996 attracted new collectors to the hobby: Topps's Mickey Mantle retrospective inserts in both series of Topps Baseball, and Leaf's Signature Series, which included one certified autograph per pack. While the Mantle craze following his passing in 1995 seemed to be a short-term phenomenon, the inclusion of autographs in packs was a trend with more long-term significance. In 1997 the print runs in selected sets got even lower. Both Fleer/SkyBox and Pinnacle Brands issued cards of which only one copy existed, known as *one-of-ones*. The growth in popularity of autographs also continued, and many products included autographed cards in their packs.

Another very positive trend was a return to basics. Many collectors bought Rookie Cards and worked on finishing sets. There was also an increase in international player collecting. Hideo Nomo was incredibly popular in Japan, while Chan Ho Park was popular in

Korea. This boded well for the prospect of international growth in the hobby. Also in 1997, Leaf introduced baseball's first game-worn memorabilia cards, incorporating company spokesman Frank Thomas's game-worn hat, jersey, batting glove, bat, and sweatband in the revolutionary Leaf Frank Thomas Collection.

1998 was a year of rebirth and growth for the hobby. The biggest boosts came from the home run race between Mark McGwire and Sammy Sosa and the continued brilliance of stalwarts like Ken Griffey Jr. and Roger Clemens. The baseball card hobby received a great deal of positive publicity from the public's renewed interest in the game. Rookie Cards featuring 1998's key players made significant gains in value as Rookie Cards once again became the collectible of choice. Both older and newer cards professionally graded by companies such as PSA and SGC also became more heavily traded. In addition, the Internet and various services such as eBay contributed to the strong growth in collecting interest during the year.

However, 1998 did have its downsides. Pinnacle Brands folded, leaving a legacy of innovation and creative promotions unmatched by the remaining companies. In addition, collectors remained frustrated by the fact that cards of their favorite players were extremely short-printed, making set completion almost impossible. During 1998, Pacific received a full baseball license and added many innovations to the card market. At the time of its release, for example, Pacific's 1998 OnLine set was the most comprehensive set issued to date, a fact that earned the applause of many veteran collectors. (In many sets produced since 1998, however, card companies have printed specific subsets—usually featuring young players—or Rookie Cards in shorter supply than regular cards.)

In 1999, many of the trends of the previous couple of years continued to gain strength. Buying, selling, and trading cards over the Internet became a dominant practice in the secondary market. EBay continued to flourish, while many other parties including Beckett Media began to reap the benefits of the burgeoning online auction and resale market. The famed Barry

Halper collection was auctioned off, bringing many museum-quality items to the market and giving the older memorabilia market a significant boost as many treasures were made available to collectors. Also, the boom in Internet trading created a perfect market for professionally graded cards, as buyers and sellers traded cards sight unseen with the confidence established by third-party graders. From a field of almost a dozen contenders, three companies emerged in 1999 to dominate the field of professional grading: Beckett Grading Services (BGS), Professional Sports Authenticator (PSA), and Sportscard Guaranty, LLC (SGC).

As had been the case in 1998, four licensed manufacturers (Fleer/SkyBox, Pacific, Topps, and Upper Deck) produced slightly more than fifty different products for 1999. Perhaps the biggest hit of the 1999 card season was created by Topps: Card #220 of the basic-issue first series, which featured home run king Mark McGwire in seventy variations, one for each homer he slugged in 1998. Many collectors went after the whole set. Continuing a legacy as strong as that of the Yankees, the basic Topps issue was one of the most popular sets released in 1999. Closely trailing the Topps McGwire promotion was Upper Deck's dynamic bat card promotion, titled "A Piece of History." The card that kicked off the frenzy was the Babe Ruth A Piece of History card, distributed in 1999 Upper Deck Series 1 packs. To create the now-famous Ruth bat card, Upper Deck actually purchased a cracked, game-used Babe Ruth bat for $24,000 and proceeded to cut it up into 350 to 400 chips of wood. The card instantly created wildly divergent opinions among hobbyists. Traditional collectors howled at the sacrilegious act of destroying such a historic piece of memorabilia, while other collectors jumped at the opportunity to chase such an important card. Upper Deck followed its Ruth card with the cross-brand "500 Club" bat card promotion, whereby it produced bat cards for every major-league ballplayer who hit 500 or more home runs in his career—except for Mark McGwire, who hit his 500th in the midst of the 1999 season, but stated that he did not support Upper Deck's promotion. (However, McGwire later agreed to the project, and a card was produced as part of the set.)

In 1999, more memorabilia cards than ever were offered to collectors as Fleer/SkyBox increased its efforts to match the standards set by Upper Deck in previous years. Batting gloves, hats, and shoes joined the typical bats and jerseys as pieces of game-used equipment featured in trading card packages. Sets like E-X Century Authen-Kicks and Fleer Mystique Feel the Game typified the new offerings. Topps only dabbled with memorabilia cards in 1999, but continued to offer some of the hottest autographed inserts, highlighted by the Topps Stars Rookie Reprint Autographs and the Topps Nolan Ryan Autographs. Pacific made a clear decision to steer clear of memorabilia and autograph inserts, instead focusing on a wide selection of beautifully designed insert and parallel cards. This continued Pacific's established precedent of making comprehensive sets, offering collectors the popular challenge of pursuing regional stars and favorite teams in addition to the typical superstars. An astounding total of 264 players made their first appearances on major-league-licensed trading cards in 1999, including a deep class of players appearing on Rookie Cards such as Adam Dunn, Josh Beckett, Pat Burrell, C. C. Sabathia, Corey Patterson, and Alfonso Soriano.

As in years past, Topps continued to provide collectors with a fistful of Rookie Cards within its Bowman, Bowman Chrome, and Bowman's Best brands. In a trend established in 1998 by Fleer when it released the Fleer Update set, hobbyists enjoyed a bevy of late-season sets chock full of RCs. Fleer/SkyBox made an all-out effort by stuffing more than 100 Rookie Cards into its 1999 Fleer Update set. Topps produced its first boxed Traded set since 1994. Each 1999 Topps Traded set contained one of seventy-five different cards autographed by a rookie prospect.

The year 2000 was marked by several major developments that would continue shaping the future of the hobby. First, Pacific decided to forfeit its baseball card license on January 1, 2000, in an effort to focus its production expenditures on football and hockey. In a separate development, Wizards of the Coast (primarily known for its non-sport gaming cards) was granted a license to produce baseball trading cards and debuted its MLB Showdown brand. These cards proved to be quite successful in that they were collected as a set by veteran collectors and played as a game by children (and some adults) both inside and outside of the traditional collecting community. By year's end, Fleer phased out its SkyBox and Flair brand names in an effort to take full advantage of the historic significance and brand recognition of its flagship Fleer sets, which were issued sporadically during the late 1950s through the 1970s and consistently from 1981 to the present.

Almost sixty brands of MLB-licensed cards, issued by five manufacturers, were produced in 2000. In addition, Just Minors and Team Best produced a variety of attractive minor league products. Most shop owners continued to generate their income primarily through the sale of packs and boxes of new products, and, as in years past, they had to make careful decisions about what to keep in stock and what to pass up for fear of a low sell-through. Vintage (or retro-themed) sets dominated the market and enabled manufacturers to tap into a base of wealthy older consumers. Game-used memorabilia cards became more abundant in all products, to the point where a few early 2001 releases included them at a rate of one per pack. The effect of this phenomenon on secondary-market values of game-used memorabilia cards has been dramatic. For example, an Alex Rodriguez or Ken Griffey Jr. game bat or game jersey card that sold for $200 in 1999 could be had for as little as $25 to $50 in early 2001. Patch cards (cards featuring swatches of jersey containing part of a multicolored patch) really caught on by year's end as the market formalized premium values on these cards.

The year 2001 was also an important one for the hobby, as it marked the largely embraced return of

Donruss to the baseball market following a two-year hiatus. Playoff, formerly a football-only manufacturer, purchased the rights to Donruss, Leaf, and Score during Pinnacle Brands' bankruptcy selloff, but wasn't awarded licenses by Major League Baseball Properties and the Major League Baseball Players Association until 2001. Today Donruss Playoff is no longer producing baseball cards, as their properties license was not renewed in December 2005.

Over the last several years, manufacturers have continued to adjust to an ever-changing marketplace, collectively delivering a splendid array of game-used memorabilia and certified autograph cards to a base of collectors who have come to expect them in seemingly every product. Breakout rookies such as Albert Pujols and Ichiro Suzuki in 2001, Mark Prior in 2002, and Dontrelle Willis in 2003 continued to ignite the Rookie Card market, and the history-chasing antics of Barry Bonds continued to make hobby headlines in 2003. In the latter part of 2003, Donruss raised the historic, game-worn memorabilia bar—and generated national media attention—by purchasing one of three remaining Babe Ruth pinstriped Yankees jerseys for more than $250,000 and holding a press conference in New York City at which Ruth's daughter, Julia Ruth Stevens, made the first cut. Since then, the four biggest manufacturers (Donruss Playoff, Fleer, Topps, and Upper Deck) have continued to release a full roster of products earmarked by requisite doses of game-used memorabilia, autographs, and deep rookie content, and featuring a healthy mix of retired players.

Top Baseball Cards

Pre-1900

1887 N172 Old Judge Cap Anson
Baseball's first superstar player, pictured on one of the very first mainstream sports card issues.

1900–1910

1909 T204 Ramly Walter Johnson
The "Big Train" in the prime of his life.

1909–11 T206 Ty Cobb (green portrait)
Any of the four Cobb cards in the T206 set are great cards, but the green portrait is clearly the toughest to find.

1909–11 T206 Sherry Magie (error)
In the first printing of Magee's card, his name was misspelled as "Magie." It was corrected very early, making the error card a true rarity.

1909–11 T206 Christy Mathewson (portrait, white cap, dark cap)
The three T206 Mathewson cards capture a national star in the prime of his youth. The portrait image is a classic for the ages.

1909–11 T206 Eddie Plank
Extremely tough-to-find card for this Hall of Famer, because it's believed that most of the Plank cards in this series suffered damage from a faulty printing plate. Those damaged cards were likely tossed out.

1909–11 T206 Honus Wagner
The most famous baseball card ever is also one of the most difficult to find. Probably less than a hundred exist, but they still find their way to auction from time to time.

1909–11 T206
Cy Young

1909–11 T206 Cy Young (portrait, white cap, dark cap)
The most famous pitcher in baseball history—he's got an award named for him, after all—appears on three different T206 cards. As with Mathewson, the portrait card is the most sought after.

1910s

1912 T207 Buck Weaver
Until his death in 1956, Weaver maintained his innocence regarding the conspiracy among gamblers and a group of Chicago White Sox players to "throw" the 1919 World Series. Weaver never accepted money and played to win in the Series, but was lumped in with the others simply for knowing what was going on around him. Weaver isn't pictured on many cards, and this is his most famous.

1914–15 Cracker Jack Ty Cobb #30
An outstanding card featuring an outstanding hitter. Visually, this is one of Cobb's most attractive issues.

1914–15 Cracker Jack Joe Jackson #103
One of the game's greatest hitters, "Shoeless" Joe Jackson may be best known as one of the eight men banned from baseball for alleged roles in the 1919 Black Sox scandal. This isn't Shoeless Joe's first card, but it is his most recognizable.

1916 M101–5 Sporting News Joe Jackson #86
This black-and-white issue was produced on the heels of Jackson's Cracker Jack card, but doesn't hold the same visual appeal. Still, it identifies him as a member of the team that made him infamous: the Chicago White Sox.

1916 M101–5 Sporting News Babe Ruth #151
The Rookie Card of the game's greatest player also happens to capture the Bambino in a Red Sox uniform—that is, "pre-curse" (before he moved to the New York Yankees).

1920s

1921 Neilson's Chocolate Babe Ruth #37
One of the Babe's very first Yankees cards, issued just a year after the trade from Boston.

1921 Neilson's Chocolate Rogers Hornsby #81
History suggests that "the Rajah" was the greatest right-handed hitter ever. This is one of Hornsby's earliest—and most significant—cards.

1930s

1932 U.S. Caramel Lou Gehrig #26
Gehrig's first mainstream card features a young-looking "Iron Horse."

1932 U.S. Caramel Babe Ruth #32
A tough card of a tough out.

1933 DeLong Lou Gehrig #7
DeLong produced just one set, but this Gehrig card makes it a memorable release.

1933 Goudey Jimmy Foxx #29 and #154
Two versions of this card exist, both featuring a similar image. For the record, the #29 is recognized as the tougher-to-find of the two and commands a higher price. But a collector couldn't go wrong with either.

1933 Goudey Babe Ruth #53 (yellow background)
Fans buying Goudey Gum cards back in 1933 had four Ruth cards to chase. Not a bad deal. Of the four, this yellow-background card is considered the toughest to find.

1933 Goudey Lou Gehrig #92 and #160
Like Foxx, Gehrig also has two cards in the 1933 Goudey set, and they resemble each other. Either one is a great addition to any collection.

1933 Goudey Napoleon Lajoie #106
A great card, and one of the toughest-to-find baseball cards of any player not named "Honus Wagner." Goudey did not print a card #106 in 1933 (was this a mistake, or a brilliant marketing plan aimed at increasing sales?), but it finally delivered the missing card a year later, in 1934. The card was available through a mail-in offer, meaning that many of these cards never found their way into collectors' hands and were probably destroyed.

1933 Goudey Hack Wilson #211
The best card featuring the man who still holds the MLB record of 191 RBI in a single season.

1933 Goudey Sport Kings Ty Cobb #1
Goudey's Sport Kings release featured Cobb as card #1 in the set.

1933 Goudey Sport Kings Babe Ruth #2
Released during Ruth's playing days, this is the most popular card in the entire Sport Kings set.

1932 U.S. Caramel Lou Gehrig #26

1941 Play Ball
Joe DiMaggio
#71

1934 Goudey Lou Gehrig #37 and #61
Goudey employed Gehrig as a company spokesman in 1934, creating two different cards of the Iron Horse, both with the same value.

1934 Goudey Hank Greenberg #62
A look at a young Hank Greenberg, just one year after he was called to the big leagues.

1936 World Wide Gum Joe DiMaggio #51
Not the prettiest card you've ever seen, but as Joltin' Joe's first national issue, it's certainly one of the most historic.

1938 Goudey Heads Up Joe DiMaggio #250
The year Goudey issued this card, DiMaggio hit .324 with 32 HR and 140 RBI, and added 13 triples for good measure. Big year. Big card.

1938 Goudey Heads Up Bob Feller #264
Goudey produced two versions of each card in the Heads Up set—one with cartoons along the sides of the card and one without—including this card, the first featuring "Rapid Robert."

1939 Play Ball Joe DiMaggio #26
Play Ball was an important brand just before the start of World War II, and its first effort featured DiMaggio on card #26. This card was released the year Joltin' Joe won the first of his three MVP awards.

1939 Play Ball Ted Williams #92
Not the most attractive card of the "Splendid Splinter," but there's no mistaking the importance of this card: it's Williams's first, issued during his rookie season.

1940s

1940 Play Ball Joe DiMaggio #1
Gum Inc., makers of the Play Ball set, knew exactly who should be featured on card #1 in its 1940 set: the "Yankee Clipper."

1940 Play Ball Ted Williams #27
Just the second mainstream Ted Williams card issued during the early part of his career, and the last black-and-white one.

1940 Play Ball "Shoeless" Joe Jackson #225
Some twenty years after the banishment from baseball of Jackson and seven teammates, it's interesting that Gum Inc. still thought enough of Jackson to include him in its regular set.

1941 Play Ball Ted Williams #14
The card collectors were pulling from packs as Williams was hitting his way to a .406 average in 1941.

1941 Play Ball Pee Wee Reese #54
The most important Rookie Card in the 1941 Play Ball set.

1941 Play Ball Joe DiMaggio #71
The card that collectors were pulling from packs as DiMaggio strung together his fifty-six-game hitting streak in 1941.

1948 Bowman Yogi Berra #6
Yogi's Rookie Card, and the start of a run in which Berra appeared on a baseball card every year through 1964.

1948 Bowman Warren Spahn #18
The Rookie Card of baseball's all-time winningest left-hander.

1948 Bowman Stan Musial #36
One of the classiest men ever to play the game, Musial made his baseball card debut with this issue in 1948.

1949 Bowman Jackie Robinson #50
One of two Robinson Rookie Cards, the Bowman isn't quite as condition sensitive as the more pricey Leaf card.

1949 Bowman Roy Campanella #84
Campy, along with Jackie Robinson and Satchel Paige, was a pioneer of the game. He also played a key role in securing the Brooklyn Dodgers' only World Series title, in 1955. This is his lone Rookie Card.

1949 Bowman Satchel Paige #224
A second Rookie Card featuring this Hall-of-Fame pitcher and true character of the game.

1949 Bowman Duke Snider #226
The "Duke of Flatbush," as he appeared on his 1949 Rookie Card.

1949 Leaf Joe DiMaggio #1
The first card in the first color set of the postwar card releases.

1949 Leaf Babe Ruth #3
Released right around the time of Ruth's death, this Leaf card remains extremely popular with collectors.

1949 Leaf Stan Musial #4
An early, colorful card of "the Man."

1953 Topps
Jackie
Robinson #1

1949 Leaf Leroy Paige
#8
*Satchel's Rookie Card
is a short print, mean-
ing that demand for
this card greatly out-
strips supply.*

1949 Leaf John Wag-
ner #70
*Honus Wagner, listed
under his real name of
"John."*

1949 Leaf Ted
Williams #76
*Teddy Ballgame just
missed the Triple
Crown in 1949, leading*

1955 Topps
Sandy Koufax
#123

*the league in HR (43) and RBI (159) but falling just short of
league best with a .343 batting average.*

1949 Leaf Jackie Robinson #79
A most important Rookie Card of a most important man.

1950s

1950 Bowman Ted Williams #98
*Bowman had been producing cards for a couple of years be-
fore it finally produced this card, the first Bowman Ted
Williams card.*

1951 Bowman Whitey Ford #1
*In the 1951 set, Bowman showcased the "Chairman of the
Board" in its place of honor: card #1.*

1951 Bowman Mickey Mantle #253
Not his most famous card, but the only true Rookie Card of the Mick.

1951 Bowman Willie Mays #305
The best card of arguably the game's best-ever all-around player.

1952 Bowman Mickey Mantle #101
Not as popular as Mantle's 1952 Topps card, but still a very important card in terms of hobby history.

1952 Bowman Willie Mays #218
Bowman placed Mays's card in its high series (or second series) in 1952, making it tougher to find than other early Mays cards, including his 1952 Topps issue.

1952 Topps Andy Pafko #1
As card #1, Pafko leads off the industry's most important postwar baseball card set: 1952 Topps. That's a big deal to a whole lot of collectors.

1952 Topps Willie Mays #261
The first Topps card featuring the "Say Hey Kid" is one of the Hall-of-Famer's best.

1952 Topps Mickey Mantle #311
This card is often mistaken for a Rookie Card, but it's not. What it is, however, is no less impressive: It's the first Topps Mantle card and one of the most popular baseball cards ever produced.

1952 Topps Jackie Robinson #312
This card appeared in the 1952 high-number series (with Mantle), making this arguably Robinson's toughest-to-find mainstream card and the subject of much attention from dedicated set builders.

1952 Topps Eddie Mathews #407
A member of the 500 Home Run Club, Mathews appears on this 407th and last card in the 1952 Topps set.

1953 Bowman Color Stan Musial #32
This card was the last that collectors saw of Musial for some time. After this card was released, Stan the Man did not appear on another major manufacturer's issue for five years.

1953 Bowman Color Pee Wee Reese #33
One of the modern hobby's first horizontal cards, and certainly one of its most attractive. This card carries the image of a Hall of Famer and is considered one of the best-looking cards ever produced.

1953 Bowman Color Mickey Mantle #59
In terms of collector popularity, this card takes a backseat to Mantle's 1953 Topps card. But with its crisp photo and blue-sky background, this card takes a backseat to no other Mantle card in terms of sheer photographic artistry.

1953 Topps Jackie Robinson #1
This is card #1 in the series and features a great image of Robinson with the Brooklyn Bridge painted behind him.

1953 Topps Mickey Mantle #82
The Mick's second Topps card is a beauty.

1953 Topps Satchel Paige #220
Paige's last card issued during his active playing days, and the only one that pictures him with the now-defunct St. Louis Browns.

1953 Topps Willie Mays #244
Topps stuck Willie in the tough high-number series in 1953, meaning that many collectors were already thinking about football cards by the time it was released. Those who do have this card appreciate it for the player it depicts and the great full-body imagery of the era it represents.

1954 Bowman Ted Williams #66A
A rare card of a rare ballplayer. Bowman pulled this Williams card shortly after production for contractual reasons, and replaced it with a card of fellow Red Sox outfielder Jimmy Piersall.

1954 Topps Ted Williams #1 and #250
With Williams finally signed to a Topps contract, the company used Teddy Ballgame to open the set and close it.

1954 Topps Ernie Banks #94
He never won a world championship with the Cubs, but Banks brought a lot of class to the North Side and drilled 512 home runs. This is his Rookie Card.

1954 Topps Hank Aaron #128
Barry Bonds may be moving up the all-time home run list, but nobody—nobody!—will ever replace Hank Aaron in the history of the game. This is the Hammer's only Rookie Card.

1954 Topps Al Kaline #201
Kaline remains the youngest player ever to win a batting championship, winning the 1955 title at age twenty. The Hall of Famer also finished his career with more than 3,000 hits.

1955 Topps Sandy Koufax #123
It's hard to believe that the youngster pictured on this card would go on to become one of the most dominant left-handers ever.

1955 Topps Harmon Killebrew #124
Killebrew was one of the game's most prolific power hitters, and his 573 home runs still rank in the top eight on the all-time home run list.

1955 Topps Roberto Clemente #164
Clemente was a complete ballplayer, and cracked his

3,000th hit in his final game before his untimely death. He accomplished plenty during his life, leaving behind a legacy of compassion and determination that continues to draw fans and collectors to this historical rookie card.

1956 Topps Mickey Mantle #135
The Mick was all smiles during his Triple Crown season of 1956. That's a pretty good catch depicted in the background of this card, too.

1957 Topps Ted Williams #1
Another significant card #1, as it features Ted Williams and it's from a set that featured the first standard 2-1/2 x 3-1/2–inch card sizes.

1961 Topps Roger Maris #2

1957 Topps Don Drysdale #18
The first look for card collectors at the second part of the Dodgers' devastating Koufax-Drysdale tandem.

1957 Topps Frank Robinson #35
Robinson won MVP awards in both leagues—he was the NL Rookie of the Year in 1956—and became baseball's first black manager during the 1970s. This Rookie Card pictures him around the time he was nailing the ROY award.

1957 Topps Brooks Robinson #328
The Human Vacuum Cleaner's first card can be found in Topps's 1957 semi–high-number series.

1958 Topps Stan Musial All-Star #476
Not a difficult card to find at all, especially since it was triple-printed. It is significant as Topps's first Stan Musial card.

1959 Fleer Ted Williams "Ted Signs for 1959" #68
Rather than risk a lawsuit from Topps (which held the rights to Bucky Harris, who appears on this card with Williams), Fleer simply removed the card from production. But not, of course, before some mint copies found their way onto the market.

1959 Topps Bob Gibson #514
Difficult-to-find high-number card that is also tough to find perfectly centered. Pink isn't exactly the color we would have picked for Gibson's Rookie Card, but who's complaining?

1960s

1960 Topps Carl Yastrzemski #148
By 1960, Topps was creating special Rookie "subsets" within their basic sets. As it turned out, the biggest star from those

1960 Rookie Stars was a 20-year-old whose career would become the baseball version of the Energizer Bunny—it kept going and going and going.

1961 Topps Roger Maris #2

Maris will always be remembered for his sixty-one home runs in 1961. In 1961, our nation was concerned not so much with the politics of the times as with which New York Yankee was going to break the immortal Babe Ruth's single-season home run record: Mickey Mantle or Roger Maris. The answer, of course, was Maris. This was the card kids were collecting that summer.

1961 Topps Juan Marichal #417

In the innocent days of card collecting, Topps would entice kids to keep buying packs by printing some cards in smaller quantities than other cards in the set. The 1961 Juan Marichal was one such card. It was more of an annoyance than anything else, because back in 1961 Marichal was just another guy needed to complete a set.

1962 Topps Mickey Mantle #200

A beautiful yet simple card featuring the Mick in the midst of what would be his final MVP season—and, not coincidentally, the last year for more than a decade in which the Yankees would win a World Series.

1963 Fleer Maury Wills #43

Topps had everyone back in the early '60s . . . well, almost everyone. They didn't have Maury Wills signed to a contract. In one of the few attempts to compete with Topps, Fleer created a set of current players packaged with a "lemon cookie" in their packs. The reviews of the cookies are still negative, but there is nothing but positive things to say about Wills—and about one of the few Wills cards issued during the first nine years of his career.

1963 Topps Pete Rose #537

Love him? Hate him? Does it matter? Those 4,256 hits and countless appearances in the postseason are all that really matter to most fans following the sport.

1963 Topps Willie Stargell #553

Like the Rose card, this issue is part of the tough 1963 high-number final series. Stargell was extremely respected for his leadership abilities and became an icon in Pittsburgh after the unfortunate passing of Roberto Clemente. There was something appropriate and sad about Stargell's dying on the very day (April 9, 2001) that a statue of him was unveiled at Pittsburgh's newly opened PNC Park.

1964 Topps Phil Niekro #541
The last member of the Milwaukee Braves to stay active in the majors, Hall-of-Famer "Knucksie" pitched until his mid-forties. This card hails from the tough high-number series and is not seen as often as other cards in the set.

1965 Topps Steve Carlton #477
"Lefty" won four Cy Young awards and was still throwing that devastating slider nearly two decades after the release of this card. For some players, talking to the media furthers their careers. For Carlton, not talking might have been the key.

1966 Topps Jim Palmer #126
Just Jim Palmer's luck that his underwear modeling gigs may have brought him more attention than his Hall-of-Fame career. Palmer was good, very good, winning World Series games in the 1960s, 1970s, and 1980s.

1967 Topps Tom Seaver #581
The current rage among Moneyball executives is to find pro-ready college pitchers. Here's one of the first modern examples of a pro-ready college pitcher. Seaver needed just a little less than one full minor-league season before moving up to the majors.

1968 Topps Nolan Ryan #177
Who could have known that the baby-faced kid on this card would become the most dominant strikeout pitcher in major league history? No one, that's who.

1968 Topps Johnny Bench #247
Bench was, and still is, considered one of the top five catchers in history, with a blend of potent bat, great glove, and powerful throwing arm.

1969 Topps Reggie Jackson #260
Somehow, Topps missed including Jackson in its 1968 set. But this 1969 card offers a great look at slugger Reginald Martinez Jackson—about eight years before anyone ever heard of a "Reggie Bar."

1969 Topps Mickey Mantle #500
The back of this card states, "Mickey announced his retirement from baseball on March 1, 1969." And thus, the "Commerce Comet" finally flamed out. For card collectors really wanting a challenge, find the Mantle card featuring his last name in white letters.

1970S

1970 Topps Thurman Munson #189
This isn't exactly a tough card to find, but it's one that continues to attract strong demand from fans wanting to remember Munson as a hard-nosed leader of the Yankees.

1975 Topps
George Brett
#228

1972 Topps 1972 Rookie Stars Red Sox (Carlton Fisk) #79
Hall-of-Famer Fisk was a rarity—a catcher who could hit, and who out-witted Father Time by catching games in four decades.

1972 Topps Steve Carlton #751
Before boxed Traded sets, Topps fig-ured the best way to document player movement—and "movement" meant only trades in those days—was to stamp information about it across the fronts of late-series cards. It was a good call by Topps to include Carlton in this seven-card subset: Lefty won twenty-seven games that season.

1973 Topps Roberto Clemente #50
This is Clemente's final regular-issue card. He died in a plane crash on December 31, 1972—just shortly before the release of this card.

1973 Topps Mike Schmidt #615
This card features Michael Jack Schmidt as he appeared be-fore hitting 500-plus home runs, garnering All-Century Team honors, and being inducted into the Hall of Fame.

1974 Topps Dave Winfield #456
Winfield entered the Hall of Fame as a member of the Padres, with whom he is pictured here—despite playing in a World Series with the New York Yankees and winning one with the Toronto Blue Jays.

1975 Topps Robin Yount #223
Yount won MVP awards at two demanding positions: short-stop and centerfield. He also collected more than 3,000 hits and entered the Hall of Fame with the outstanding Class of 1999: Nolan Ryan, George Brett, and Orlando Cepeda.

1975 Topps George Brett #228
There was only one George Howard Brett, and for twenty-one seasons he could be counted on to put forth a maximum effort each and every day he stepped onto the field. That kind of commitment to the game carried him directly to Cooperstown.

1978 Topps Eddie Murray #36
Cal Ripken Jr. credits Murray's work ethic as one of the pri-mary inspirations for his famous consecutive-games-played streak. This card is known for being tough to find in perfect condition, and there is a premium on well-centered issues.

1978 Topps Paul Molitor #707
One of the four players on this card—Molitor—is already in the Hall of Fame. It's not a stretch to suggest that another, former Tigers shortstop Alan Trammell, could sometime join him. Two Hall of Famers on one card? How cool is that?

1979 Topps Ozzie Smith #116
Ozzie may have been the leading defensive shortstop wizard of this, or any other, generation. But even his wizardry couldn't make this card come out of the packs well centered. Find a perfectly centered copy, and you've really got something valuable.

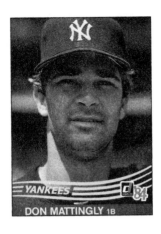

1984 Donruss
Don Mattingly
#248

1980s

1980 Topps Rickey Henderson #482
The greatest leadoff hitter in the history of the game, Henderson played during four decades before finishing as the game's all-time leader in stolen bases, walks, and runs scored.

1981 Topps Dodgers Future Stars (Fernando Valenzuela) #302
Back in 1981 at the height of "Fernandomania," this card was about as coveted as a baseball card can get.

1982 Topps Baltimore Orioles Future Stars (Cal Ripken Jr.) #21
Topps's first look at Ripken included two other prospects as well. Only the "Iron Man" made a name for himself from the trio. And what a name it was.

1982 Topps Traded Cal Ripken Jr. #98T
Ripken's first solo card produced by Topps happens to be a beauty, and without question his most important mainstream card.

1983 Topps Ryne Sandberg #83
Enshrined in the Hall of Fame, Sandberg was a power-hitting second baseman before that type of player came into vogue (hello, Alfonso Soriano), and was pure gold in the field—as his nine Gold Glove awards prove.

1983 Topps Tony Gwynn #482
It seems only natural that Gwynn's Topps Rookie Card pictures him legging out a base hit.

1983 Topps Wade Boggs #498
Back in 1983, collectors speculating on this Boggs Rookie Card figured a bright future lay ahead for the third baseman. They just didn't know how bright: a .328 lifetime average, 3,010 hits, and five batting titles.

1984 Donruss Don Mattingly #248
This card—although it doesn't bring the secondary market prices that it once did—still is recognized as cardboard royalty. This Mattingly Rookie Card provided a major boost to the card collecting industry during the 1980s, and helped a new generation of collectors understand the principles of supply and demand.

1984 Fleer Update Roger Clemens #U27
The first MLB-licensed card featuring "the Rocket"; no other company included the Red Sox prospect in a 1984 set.

1984 Fleer Update Dwight Gooden #U43
Gooden exploded onto the baseball scene in 1984, finishing the season with a rookie record 276 strikeouts. His cards—the few that were available—were huge. This was easily the biggest of the bunch.

1984 Fleer Update Kirby Puckett #U93
Fleer was the first out of the gate with a Puckett card, including the Hall of Famer in its 1984 Update set.

1985 Topps Roger Clemens #181
The first Topps card featuring Clemens, and a key card for any Topps collector.

1985 Topps Mark McGwire #401
During Big Mac's home run barrage of 1998, this card took on a life of its own and in some cases was trading for more than $200. Its value has stabilized since McGwire's retirement, but it's still one of the key cards of the decade.

1986 Donruss Jose Canseco #39
Once a $100 card featuring a perceived future Hall of Famer; now a $10 card featuring a guy who hit a few home runs but will have to fight the crowds and stand in the ticket line to enter the Hall of Fame.

1986 Fleer Update Barry Bonds #14
As with other Bonds cards from the mid-1980s, this card has benefited from Bonds's trek up the all-time home run list.

1986 Topps Traded Barry Bonds #11T
The first Topps-produced Bonds card has been popular with collectors because of its plentiful supply, which has translated into an affordable price.

1987 Donruss Greg Maddux #36
Another condition-sensitive card—black borders often create this problem—and one of which centered copies are few and far between.

1987 Fleer Barry Bonds #604
Another important Bonds card from among his early cards; this was considered the crown jewel of Bonds's 1987 releases and can be difficult to find in Gem Mint condition due to its blue borders.

1989 Donruss Baseball's Best Sammy Sosa #324
Sammy as a Ranger? This must make Texas fans cringe.

1993 SP Derek Jeter #279

1989 Upper Deck Ken Griffey Jr. #1
The first card of a benchmark set, the Griffey Upper Deck Rookie Card helped usher in a new era of "premium brand" Rookie Card collecting.

1989 Upper Deck Randy Johnson #25
The "Big Unit" pictured on his Rookie Card long before anyone, anywhere had ever referred to him as the "Big Unit."

1990s

1990 Leaf Sammy Sosa #220
You won't find too many cards that show Sammy laying down a bunt. But here's one.

1990 Leaf Frank Thomas #300
The 1990 Leaf set, like 1989 Upper Deck, was considered a premium-card release and was bought and sold as such. At the time, Big Frank was the Big Card.

1990 Upper Deck Reggie Jackson Autograph #AU1
By inserting 2,500 signed Reggie Jackson cards into the set, Upper Deck introduced what would become an important part of collecting today: certified autographs.

1991 Bowman Chipper Jones #569
Jones has been an outstanding ballplayer for several years now—some might even say he's building a Hall of Fame career. If so, they'll look back and see this as his most desirable first card.

1992 Bowman Mike Piazza #461
Piazza's Rookie Card—the only Piazza card you could get out of a pack in 1992—helped establish Bowman as a brand offering products brimming with key Rookie Cards.

1992 Fleer Update Mike Piazza #92

Fleer didn't get the initial orders for which they had hoped, and so the 1992 Update Set was printed in limited quantities. That would have been fine. But after Piazza began smashing baseballs on a regular basis, everyone wanted a set.

1992 Topps Traded Nomar Garciaparra #39T

The only way collectors could get this card was to buy the entire Topps Traded box set. Those who did know they made a good move.

1993 SP Derek Jeter #279

Five World Series rings and a lifetime .316 average make Jeter more than just your run-of-the-mill shortstop. And this is far greater than just your run-of-the-mill Rookie Card.

1994 SP Alex Rodriguez #15

A-Rod has come a long way since posing for this card photo more than ten years ago. Rodriguez has a handful of Rookie Cards, but this is without question the most important of the lot—a card that should continue to gain prominence now that A-Rod is in New York.

1996 Leaf Signature Series Extended Sammy Sosa Autograph SP/1000

Donruss/Leaf introduced the one-autograph-per-pack concept to the baseball card industry in the mid-1990s, and although not necessarily cost effective from a business standpoint, it did catch collectors' attention. So did this Sammy autograph.

1997 Upper Deck Game Jersey Ken Griffey Jr. #GJ1

With so many jersey cards released today, it seems as if the concept has been around forever. But it hasn't. The concept was introduced by Upper Deck in 1997, and this card featuring a swatch of Griffey's green Mariners jersey was at the forefront of the trend.

1999 Upper Deck A Piece of History Babe Ruth Bat #P

Simply one of the most controversial cards ever, but one that will always have historical significance. Many were outraged when UD sliced and diced a game-used Ruth bat, but once the dust settled, collectors began to see the card for what it really was: the first opportunity for many to actually own, as the series title suggested, a piece of history.

2000s

2001 Bowman Chrome Albert Pujols #340
Pujols's card has all the ingredients of an important card: it's autographed, it's a Rookie Card, and it features one of the best hitters in the game over the last five seasons. Collectors haven't been shy about shelling out big bucks for this one.

2001 SP Legendary Cuts Ty Cobb/24
The cut autographs in Legendary Cuts rank with the most important—and aesthetically pleasing—insert sets ever produced. The lineup of Hall of Famers and all-time greats is awesome, with Cobb's among the toughest cut signatures to acquire.

2001 Bowman Chrome Albert Pujols #340

2001 SPx Ichiro Suzuki JSY AU #150
The hype surrounding Ichiro during his MLB rookie season of 2001 was big, introducing Americans to one of the greatest Japanese players ever. This SPx card offered collectors a piece of game jersey, an autograph, and a limited production run.

2001 Ultimate Collection Mark Prior #116
Another autographed Rookie Card with limited production (just 250 cards were produced) and virtually unlimited demand.

2002 Bowman Chrome David Wright AU #385
New York's newest golden boy is all about the Benjamins. His only autographed RC is valued at a cool $700.

2003 Bowman's Best Ryan Howard AU #RH
Baseball's best young slugger has the only legitimate chance of threatening Barry Bonds' single-season home run record.

2004 Bowman Chrome Draft AFLAC Autographs Justin Upton #JU
This card reached $1,000 before the former number one overall draft pick had completed his first year of minor league baseball.

2005 Absolute Memorabilia Tools of the Trade Swatch Single Jumbo Babe Ruth #102
The coaster-sized jersey swatch from the Bambino's 1925 season makes this issue the most significant and influential game-used card ever produced.

8

THE HISTORY OF FOOTBALL CARDS

Until the 1930s, the only set devoted exclusively to football players was the Mayo N302 set. The first bubble gum issue dedicated entirely to football players did not appear until the National Chicle issue of 1935. Before this, athletes from several sports were pictured in the multisport Goudey Sport Kings issue of 1933. In that set, football was represented by three legends whose fame has not diminished through the years: Red Grange, Knute Rockne, and Jim Thorpe. But it was not until 1948, and the postwar bubble gum boom, that the next football issues appeared. Bowman and Leaf Gum companies both issued football card sets in that year. Since that time, football cards have been issued annually by one company or another. Topps was the only major card producer until 1989, when Pro Set and Score debuted and sparked a football card boom.

Football cards depicting players from the Canadian Football League (CFL) did not appear until Parkhurst issued a 100-card set in 1952. Four years later, Parkhurst issued another fifty-card CFL set. Topps began issuing CFL sets in 1958 and continued annually until 1965, although from 1961 to 1965 these cards were printed in Canada by O-Pee-Chee. Post Cereal issued two CFL sets in 1962 and 1963; these cards were found on the backs of boxes of Post cereals distributed in Canada. The O-Pee-Chee company, essentially a subsidiary of Topps, issued four CFL sets in the years 1968, 1970, 1971, and 1972. Since 1981, the JOGO Novelties Company has produced a number of CFL sets depicting past and present players.

With respect to American issues, Bowman resumed its football card production from 1950 to 1955, by then making cards with full-color fronts. The company increased the size of its cards twice during that period. During most of the early 1950s, Bowman was the sole producer of cards featuring pro football players. Topps issued its first football card set in 1950 with a group of very small, felt-back issues. In 1951 Topps issued what is referred to as the "Magic Football Card" set. This series of seventy-five featured cards with a scratch-off section on the back, which revealed answers to a football quiz. Topps did not issue another football set until 1955, when its landmark All-American Football set paid tribute to past college greats.

In January 1956, the Topps Gum Company purchased the Bowman Company. After the purchase, Topps issued card sets of NFL players until 1963. The 1961 Topps football set also included American Football League (AFL) players in the high-number series (133–198). Topps sets from 1964 to 1967 showcased AFL players only. Since 1968, Topps has issued at least one major set of football cards each year. When the AFL was founded in 1960, Fleer produced a 132-card set featuring AFL players and coaches. In 1961, Fleer issued a 220-card set (even larger than the Topps issue of that year) featuring players from both the NFL and AFL. For that one year, Topps and Fleer tested a reciprocal arrangement in which they traded the card printing rights to each other's contracted players. The 1962 and 1963 Fleer sets featured only AFL players. Both sets are relatively small, at eighty-eight cards each. Post Cereal's 200-card 1962 set of NFL players contains numerous scarcities, namely those players appearing on unpopular varieties of Post cereals. From 1964 to 1967, Philadelphia Gum issued four 198-card NFL player sets.

In 1984 and 1985, Topps produced a set for the now-defunct United States Football League, in addition to its annual NFL set. The 1984 set in particular is quite scarce, due both to low distribution and high demand for the extended Rookie Cards of future NFL superstars Jim Kelly and Reggie White, among others.

In 1986, McDonald's restaurants generated great excitement over football cards through a nationwide promotion in which customers could request one or two cards per food purchase. However, these cards featured local teams only—or, in areas not near NFL cities, the "McDonald's All-Stars." Also, each set was produced with four possible color tabs: blue, black, gold, or green. The tab color depended on the week of the promotion in which the card was distributed. In general, cards with blue tabs are the scarcest, although for some teams the cards with black tabs are the most difficult to find. The tabs were intended to be scratched off by customers and redeemed for food and other prizes, but among collectors, cards with scratched or removed tabs are categorized as having a major defect, and therefore are valued considerably lower. The entire set, including different color tabs for all four subsets, totals more than 2,800 different cards.

Enthusiasm about the McDonald's cards fell precipitously after 1988, when collector interest shifted to the landmark 1989 Score and Pro Set issues. Card companies other than Topps had noticed the burgeoning interest in football cards, resulting in the 330-card Score issue and the 440-card Pro Set release. Score later produced a self-contained 110-card supplemental set, while Pro Set printed 100 Series II cards and a twenty-one-card Final Update set. Topps, Pro Set, and Score all improved card quality and increased the size of their sets for 1990. That season also marked Fleer's return to football cards and the first major set from Action Packed.

In 1991, Pacific, Pro Line, Upper Deck, and Wild Card joined a market that was becoming as competitive as the market for baseball cards. And the premium card trend that began on the diamond spilled over to the gridiron in the form of Fleer Ultra, Pro Set Platinum, Score Pinnacle, and Topps Stadium Club sets. The year 1992 brought even more growth, with the debuts of All World, Collector's Edge, GameDay, Playoff, Pro Set Power, SkyBox Impact, and SkyBox Primetime.

The football card market stabilized somewhat in 1993, thanks to an agreement between the long-feuding NFL licensing bodies NFL Properties and the NFL Players Association. Furthering the stabilization was the emergence of several promising rookies, including Drew Bledsoe, Jerome Bettis, and Rick Mirer. "Limited production" became the industry buzzword in sports cards, and the football market was no exception. The result was the success of three new product lines: 1993 Playoff Contenders, 1993 Select, and 1993 SP. Pro Set and Wild Card dropped out of the market in 1994, and no new card companies joined the ranks. However, several new NFL sets were added to the mix by existing manufacturers: Classic NFL Experience, Collector's Choice, Excalibur, Finest, and Sportflics. The new trend centered on multilevel parallel sets and interactive game inserts with parallel prizes. Another strong rookie crop and reported production cutbacks contributed to strong football card sales throughout 1994. The football card market continued to grow between 1995 and 1998. Companies continued to push the limits of printing technology with issues printed on plastic, leather, cloth, and various metals. Rookie Cards once more came into vogue, and the "one-of-one" insert card was born.

In 1998, Playoff used its Contenders brand to produce the industry's first base-set cards featuring rookie autographs. Due to the complicated makeup of the set, Contenders' rookies failed to receive the Rookie Card designation from industry publications. Nonetheless, there's no denying the impact of Playoff's efforts—highlighted by cards featuring Peyton Manning and Randy Moss rookie autographs. Upper Deck took a page from Playoff's autographed-rookie-card book to set the football card world on fire with the 1998 release of SP Authentic. These were the hobby's first serial numbered Rookie Cards, numbered to 2,000 sets. The Peyton Manning, Randy Moss, and Fred Taylor RCs were the hottest cards of their time, and the Manning and Moss cards remain among the top RCs of all time. Pinnacle Brands ceased to exist in 1998, with the Playoff Company taking over the rights to produce long-standing football brands such as Score and Leaf.

1998 SP Authentic Peyton Manning RC #14

Every major company today issues game-worn memorabilia and certified autographed cards of leading players, both active and retired. The first certified autographs inserted into packs were the 1991 Upper Deck Joe Montana and Joe Namath Heroes autograph cards. Montana and Namath sighed 2,500 cards each—a huge number by today's standards. Namath even signed every 100 cards "Broadway Joe." In addition, sets such as the 1997 Upper Deck Legends Autographs and the 1999 Sports Illustrated signed cards brought the greats of the past back into collectors' eyes. These game-worn cards include swatches of jerseys, footballs, helmets, and anything else that can be used by a player during a game. Today, some companies are getting players to sign many of these cards to make them more attractive to collectors. The first game-worn jersey football cards appeared in the ten-card 1996 Upper Deck Game Jerseys set, including cards featuring all-time greats like Joe Montana, Barry Sanders, and Jerry Rice. This set is valued at around

$2,000 today. A few current card sets also include jersey swatches in some of the base cards.

In addition, graded cards—both old and new—have revitalized the card market. Many collectors and dealers have been able to buy, sell, and trade cards using Internet services such as eBay or through the various means available on Beckett.com. These cards make sight-unseen trading much easier than it used to be. Many key Rookie Cards now are issued with an autograph, uniform swatch, or even both. In addition, the print run of many of these singles is smaller each year. One example is the landmark 2001 SP Authentic Michael Vick #91, which reached an incredible value of $1,600 in 2003.

A significant number of autographs are no longer signed on actual cards, but instead are signed on stickers that are then affixed to cards. This practice is common with Donruss Playoff products, such as Playoff Contenders, and with a few Upper Deck brands. Card companies have adopted this practice to reduce the number of *redemption cards* (cards you send in to the company to receive a limited edition set) for each product.

While some collectors are frustrated by the changing hobby, others are thrilled because there are more choices than ever before for football card collectors—and many collectors like it that way.

Top Football Cards

1930s

1933 Sport Kings Jim Thorpe #6
This legendary issue captures arguably the greatest pure athlete in American history on his first football card.

1935 National Chicle Knute Rockne #9
It was a no-brainer for National Chicle to include Knute Rockne in a set otherwise exclusive to NFL players. From the day it was made, this card has been in demand, and today it still has almost fantastic significance.

1935 National Chicle Bronko Nagurski #34
Bronislau "Bronko" Nagurski was the embodiment of power when he played with the Chicago Bears in the 1930s. Today

the Bronk's Rookie Card is a momentous relic, and one of the most valuable football cards in existence.

1940s

1948 Leaf Sid Luckman #1
Leaf opted to kick off its history-making ninety-eight-card football set (which includes both pro and college players) with this Rookie Card of Luckman, another of the Bears' seemingly countless Hall of Famers during the NFL's formative years.

1948 Leaf Sammy Baugh #34
By the time Baugh's Leaf Rookie Card (which features his nickname, "Slingin' Sammy Baugh") was released in the fall of 1948, Baugh was in his twelfth NFL season, and he'd already helped the Redskins win two NFL titles.

1955 Topps
All-American
Jim Thorpe
#37

1950s

1950 Bowman Otto Graham #45
In ten professional seasons, Graham played in ten championship games. He won seven of them. His Bowman Rookie Card is the key issue in the 1950 set.

1950 Topps Felt Backs Joe Paterno #64
Even in 1950, college football was far more popular than the NFL. Topps decided to devote the second set it ever produced to college football, and chose to include the baby-faced Ivy-Leaguer Paterno, then the co-captain and quarterback for Brown University. That baby-faced QB went on to become arguably the greatest college head coach of all time.

1951 Bowman Norm Van Brocklin #4
Van Brocklin, who entered the Hall of Fame twenty years after his Rookie Card was printed, was one of the NFL's golden boys in the 1950s. He still holds the single-game passing record of 554 yards.

1951 Bowman Tom Landry #20
Tom Landry rivals Vince Lombardi and Don Shula as one of the greatest coaching minds in football history, having led the Cowboys to twenty consecutive winning seasons, five conference championships, and two Super Bowl titles.

1952 Bowman Large Jim Lansford #144
Lansford's card, the last in the set, is the shortest of all 1952 Bowman Large short prints, because it was unfortunately situated on the lower-right corner of the second production

sheet. Bowman's production equipment was unaccustomed to manufacturing larger-size cards, and most Lansfords suffered severe damage and were destroyed.

1955 Topps All-American Jim Thorpe #37
The Thorpe card is the most popular issue in one of football's most recognizable sets ever.

1955 Topps All-American Four Horsemen #68
Harry Stuhldreher, Elmer Layden, Jim Crowley, and Don Miller constituted Knute Rockne's almost-mythical backfield, and were dubbed "the Four Horsemen of the Apocalypse" by legendary sportswriter Grantland Rice because they usually caused catastrophic results for Notre Dame's opposition. All four appear on this short-printed card.

1957 Topps Bart Starr #119
Starr is just one of the all-time great quarterbacks featured on a Rookie Card in the 1957 Topps set. He remains extremely popular today, having achieved pioneering victories in the first two Super Bowls.

1957 Topps Johnny Unitas #138
Johnny U's 1957 Topps card is one of the most popular Rookie Cards in any sport. His unparalleled ability and recognizable flat-top haircut and high-top black cleats helped Unitas become an icon during his eighteen-season NFL career.

1957 Topps Paul Hornung #151
In a career laced with the kind of success typically reserved for movie characters, Hornung won the 1956 Heisman Trophy as a quarterback at Notre Dame, then entered the NFL one year later with a juggernaut Packers franchise, eventually leading the team to four NFL championships.

1958 Topps Jim Brown #62
So stunning was Brown's dominance that even now, more than thirty years after his retirement, he's still regarded by most observers as the greatest running back ever to play the game. His Rookie Card, which features the nickname "Jimmy Brown," is a classic issue.

1960s

1960 Fleer Jack Kemp #124
Rookie Cards of seventeenth-round draft picks who throw almost seventy more career interceptions (183) than touchdowns (114) typically aren't even remembered, much less revered. But Kemp's first card, it can be argued with considerable validity, is the most consequential issue Fleer ever produced.

1962 Topps Mike Ditka #17
This Rookie Card of Ditka, the first tight end ever inducted into the Hall of Fame (Class of 1988), features one of the

most attractive, condition-sensitive set designs in trading card history.

1962 Topps Fran Tarkenton #90
Tarkenton's Rookie Card actually features two Hall-of-Fame quarterbacks. The guy pictured in the black-and-white photo is an airbrushed Sonny Jurgensen, who was playing for the Eagles at the time.

1963 Fleer Len Dawson #47
In nineteen seasons of professional football, Dawson, the 1962 AFL Player of the Year and the MVP of Super Bowl IV, earned a reputation as one of the sharpest shooters in the game.

1963 Fleer Lance Alworth #72
They called him "Bambi" in a nod to Disney's animated fawn, although Alworth was blessed with the speed, fluidity, and grace of a gazelle. Alworth, whose Rookie Card seems like a bargain compared to some of today's stratospherically expensive cards, entered the Hall of Fame in 1978.

1965 Topps Joe Namath #122
Was it calculated or coincidental that Topps experimented for the first and only time with an oversized format (2-1/2 x 4-1/16) in a set that happened to include arguably the greatest football card ever made? Namath was larger than life on this card, which is one of the most coveted treasures in all of the hobby.

1965 Topps Fred Biletnikoff #133
This short-printed first card features a rare photograph of Biletnikoff with a buzz cut.

1966 Philadelphia Dick Butkus #31
Arguably the most disruptive, feared force ever to wear shoulder pads, Butkus wreaked havoc on his opponents, earning eight trips to the Pro Bowl. Butkus's simple debut card remains among the most cherished vintage issues of all time.

1966 Philadelphia Gale Sayers #38
Sayers played his rookie season as if he somehow knew his career would be cut short by knee injuries, totaling 1,374 yards from scrimmage, 898 return yards, and twenty-two total touchdowns. His RC is even more valuable than that of the legendary Walter Payton.

1966 Topps Funny Ring Checklist #15
It truly is funny (peculiar, not humorous) that the only non-football card in the 132-card 1966 Topps set is more sought after than any card from the set featuring an AFL player. Most collectors today consider it the most difficult of all 1966 Topps cards to locate in top condition.

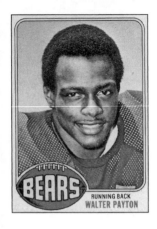

1976 Topps
Walter Payton
#148

1970s

1970 Topps O.J. Simpson #90
Simpson, the 1968 Heisman Trophy winner from USC, became the first player in NFL history to rush for more than 2,000 yards (1973) and finished his career with 11,236 yards rushing. Today, his Rookie Card is one of the better bargains in the hobby.

1971 Topps Terry Bradshaw #156
Bradshaw's Rookie Card, a red-bordered, condition-sensitive gem, is arguably the single most significant football card produced in the 1970s. Bradshaw, who was inducted into the Hall of Fame in 1989, passed for 27,989 yards and 212 touchdowns in a fourteen-year career.

1972 Topps Roger Staubach #200
Back in the day, Topps reserved card numbers such as 100, 200, and 300 for the game's premier players. Staubach certainly fits the bill. The 1985 Hall-of-Fame inductee led the Cowboys to two Super Bowl victories and finished his career with 22,700 yards passing, 2,264 yards rushing, 173 total touchdowns, and a passer rating of 83.4.

1975 Topps Lynn Swann #282
The misspelling of "reciever" on his Rookie Card didn't prevent Swann from becoming one of the most acrobatically gifted receivers in the game.

1976 Topps Walter Payton #148
"Sweetness" embodied what every team looks for in a running back, and what every fan wants in a superstar. His Rookie Card is a classy, traditional reminder of why Payton is a true hero.

1978 Topps Tony Dorsett #315
It's hard to fathom any Rookie Card representing a better value than this one. Dorsett, the former Heisman Trophy winner from Pitt, enjoyed a profusely rich Hall-of-Fame career, rushing for 12,739 yards and seventy-seven touchdowns in twelve seasons.

1979 Topps Earl Campbell #390
"The Tyler Rose" still inspires the generation of big, pounding runners we see in the NFL today. His Topps Rookie Card serves as a reminder of a young Campbell awaiting his Hall-of-Fame career.

1980s

1981 JOGO CFL B/W Warren Moon #23

Before he became one of the NFL's all-time most productive passers, Moon was breaking records north of the border for the Edmonton Eskimos. This 3-1/2 x 5–inch black-and-white card was Moon's first card of any kind, and predates his first NFL card by five years.

1981 Topps Joe Montana #216

Montana's simple first card, issued two years after he entered the league, almost single-handedly kept the football card industry afloat for the remainder of the decade, and well into the 1990s.

1984 Topps John Elway #63

One of the best all-around QBs ever to step on a field has a Rookie Card in one of the best RC sets ever.

1984 Topps Dan Marino #123

This gridiron gem supplanted Joe Montana's RC as the card to collect in the late 1980s and early 1990s, and it seemed to gain value with every passing record (Marino retired with no fewer than twenty-five of them). However, its value has faltered a bit in recent years.

1984 Topps USFL Steve Young #52

Despite missing the first five games of the 1984 season, Young led the Los Angeles Express to an 8–5 record with his trademark diversity. Young's Extended Rookie Card is now the cornerstone of a smallish 132-card offering that was released as a boxed set only.

1986 Topps Jerry Rice #161

Without question, this is the greatest receiver card in history, featuring the greatest receiver in history. A box of 1986 Topps Football cards should contain one or two Rice RCs.

1989 Score Barry Sanders #257

Sanders's best Rookie Card began an improbable climb in value and prestige during a remarkable 1997 season that saw his physical brilliance (2,053 yards, including an NFL record–breaking fourteen straight 100-yard games) meld with one of the most universally popular sports card trends in history: professional grading.

1989 Score Troy Aikman #270

Simply put, this is one of the four or five greatest football card sets ever produced, featuring no fewer than seven surefire Hall of Famers among its stellar crop of Rookie Cards. But it was this golden-boy quarterback enduring a bad-hair day who put this landmark set on the football map.

1990 Score
Supplemental
Emmitt Smith
#101T

1990s

1990 Score Supplemental Emmitt
Smith #101T
*During Dallas's reign atop the NFL
rankings in the early to mid-1990s,
Emmitt's blue-bordered Score debut
was undoubtedly the most influential,
desirable card in the sport. Score's
110-card update set was released exclusively through the company's
dealer outlets and available only as a
complete set.*

1991 Stadium Club Brett Favre #94
*OK, so someone at Topps butchered
Favre's name (spelled "Farve") the first time they had to use
it. Despite the error, this single quickly became Favre's most
traded Rookie Card in the mid-1990s.*

1996 Upper Deck Game Jersey Joe Montana #GJ3
*What Thomas Edison was to electricity, Isaac Newton was to
gravity, and the Wright Brothers were to flying, this insert set
was to the game-used memorabilia card. Today, echoes of
Upper Deck's Game Jersey concept can be seen in virtually
every card product made by every manufacturer in every
sport.*

1998 SP Authentic Peyton Manning #14
*Upper Deck's 1998 SP Authentic set introduced the ground-
breaking concept of serial-numbered Rookie Cards (in this
case numbered to 2,000). In 1998, the Manning card
seemed to climb in value by the month.*

1998 SP Authentic Randy Moss #18
*As popular as the Manning card was, Moss's issue was just
as hot. As a rookie, Moss totaled over 1,300 yards and seven-
teen TDs. Each of his catches went for an average of 19
yards, adding needed excitement to the league and the
hobby.*

1999 Donruss Elite Passing the Torch Autographs
#4A (Walter Payton and Barry Sanders)
*One of the greatest cards of 1999 provides a serendipitous
union of signatures from the two greatest running backs who
ever lived.*

1999 Upper Deck Retro Walter Payton Autographed
Game Jersey NNO
*It's an eerie coincidence that "Sweetness" finally lost his bat-
tle with cancer in a year when so many new and wonderful
Payton cards were introduced to the marketplace. But perhaps none was more compelling than this one, which combines a piece of Payton game-used jersey and Payton's
beautiful inscription on a card limited to just thirty-four
copies.*

2000s

2000 SP Authentic Tom Brady #118
*In terms of value, this has been one of the most volatile cards
of the past few years. Brady's dual Super Bowl MVP performances have helped this issue top the $800 mark.*

2001 SP Authentic Michael Vick #91
*It might seem hasty to include such a recent card on a list of
the greatest football cards of all time. However, few cards
have affected the football card industry like this Vick SP Authentic Rookie Card. Featuring a jersey patch and autograph,
and limited in quantity (250), this gem easily tops the $1,500
mark when offered for sale.*

2002 Donruss Elite Throwback Threads Jim Thorpe/Red
Grange #TT21
*Pairing the two fathers of football on one card is a great idea,
but also including game-worn memorabilia swatches is sheer
genius. This card remains one of the top inserts ever produced.*

2004 SP Authentic Ben Roethlisberger #213
*"Big Ben" solidified his marketplace stature when he became
the youngest quarterback to ever win the Super Bowl.*

2005 Exquisite Collection Cadillac Williams JSY AU RC
#117
*This card represents the next stage in the evolution of the
football Rookie Card. Upper Deck's ground-breaking Exquisite Collection product yielded the unquestioned No. 1 Rookie
Card of 2005—a dual jersey/patch autograph of 2005 Rookie
of the Year Cadillac Williams.*

2006 Donruss Threads Reggie Bush AU/100 RC #250
*Donruss introduced the first autographed nameplate letter
patch Rookie Card in 2006 Donruss Threads. The super-hot
Reggie Bush sold for upwards of $1,000 upon release.*

Autographs

What follows is a list of the ten football autographs
currently most coveted by collectors.

Jim Brown

It seems that Brown's 'graph is more attainable on certified autographed cards than on memorabilia these days. In fact, in 2002 and 2003 Brown released eleven different certified autographed cards (not including parallels).

Brett Favre

Favre autographs are never hard to find. Mini-helmets, footballs, jerseys, cards, photos—he signs 'em all.

Dan Marino

Marino has a nice-looking signature and almost always supplements it with his number, 13. Although he never won the "big one," Dan the Man holds the all-time records for passing TDs, yards, attempts, and completions.

Joe Montana

He's regarded by many as the greatest QB ever to grip the pigskin. He is also a willing signer, so there is no shortage of Montana-autographed memorabilia and cards. Montana signs a lot of merchandise for TriStar Productions, including San Francisco and Notre Dame memorabilia.

Joe Namath

Plenty of Namath items are authenticated and sold by Steiner Sports. He has a nice, flowing autograph, and some items even include his nickname, "Joe Willie Namath." Like Montana, Namath will typically sign items that represent his alma mater, Alabama.

Walter Payton

Walter Payton may boast the most beautiful signature in the history of football players. Unfortunately, "Sweetness" is no longer with us, but there are still plenty of signed items by which to remember him.

Jerry Rice

Rice is known to sign in public, but if you are never fortunate enough to score an autograph in person, a mini-helmet generally runs about $200 to $250, while a football is about $300. Both 49ers and Raiders items are readily available. Rice also appears on a huge selection of autographed cards.

Barry Sanders

There's no doubt that Sanders's early retirement added to the popularity of his autographed items. He still signs for card companies and has done a lot of signings for Schwartz Sports and TriStar. His induction into the Hall of Fame in 2004 could drive demand for his 'graph even higher.

Emmitt Smith

Like Payton, the legend whom he passed on the all-time rushing list, Smith has a beautiful and very recognizable signature. The thing to remember about Smith is that he will not sign in person memorabilia such as footballs, mini-helmets, or virtually any items with his image on them. However, he has done plenty of official signings in the past, and still signs for card companies. His autographed cards date back to the early 1990s.

Johnny Unitas

Until his death in 2002, Johnny U signed plenty of cards, some pairing him with current players such as Peyton Manning. Expect to pay no less than $100 for a certified, autographed Unitas card. Signed memorabilia is pretty tough to find, so expect to shell out the dough if you do run across some.

9
THE HISTORY OF
HOCKEY CARDS

Hockey cards have been produced for a much longer time than football or basketball cards—a fact no doubt influenced by the predominance of hockey as Canada's national pastime. Cigarette companies issued hockey cards from 1910 to 1913, but while three distinct cigarette card sets have been identified, the manufacturers of these sets are not known. During the 1920s, four candy hockey sets and one cigarette hockey set were issued, none in color. It was not until the 1930s that the Canadian gum companies started issuing card premiums with their chewing gum; World Wide Gum Co. and the familiar O-Pee-Chee were among these early issuers. Bee Hive photos, an incredibly popular food premium that lasted three decades, also made their first appearance during the 1930s.

The recent history of hockey cards begins with the post–World War II Parkhurst issues of the 1950s and

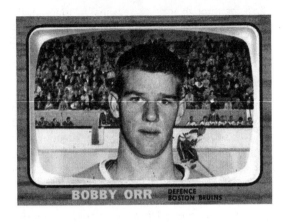

early 1960s. Parkhurst issued hockey card sets from 1951 through 1964, except during the 1956–57 season. Topps started issuing hockey cards in 1954. Then, after a two-year hiatus, it issued cards regularly from the 1957–58 season until the present, with the exception of a break during the 1982–83 and 1983–84 seasons. During the 1950s, Topps typically issued cards featuring players from American teams, while Parkhurst issued cards featuring players from the two Canadian teams existing at the time: Montreal and Toronto. From the 1960–61 season until its demise after the 1963–64 season, Parkhurst issued cards featuring players from the two Canadian teams plus Detroit, while Topps issued cards featuring players from the remaining three American teams. Beginning with the 1964–65 season, Topps issued player cards from all teams in the NHL. During the 1966–67 season, Topps attempted to produce a sixty-six-card set aimed strictly at the American market, with no French on the cards. This test issue, now quite scarce, is very similar to the regular 1966–67 Topps set and includes a key Bobby Orr card.

O-Pee-Chee re-entered the hockey card market in 1968, and has been a relative constant in the market ever since. O-Pee-Chee sets typically are larger in size than Topps sets, perhaps a reflection of the relative popularity of hockey in Canada as compared to the United States. O-Pee-Chee issued separate card sets featuring World Hockey Association players for the

1974–75 through 1977–78 seasons. In 1990–91, the NHL card market welcomed five major new sets: Bowman, O-Pee-Chee Premier, Pro Set, Score, and Upper Deck. Most of these sets represented significant improvements over the quality of previous sets, and all enjoyed moderate-to-superb levels of success, reflecting the public's growing interest in hockey cards. Score and Upper Deck issued Canadian and French sets, respectively, which drew attention from collectors due to their perceived relative scarcity. The success of Score's debut sets was partially fueled by the inclusion of a card featuring ultra-talented prospect Eric Lindros. Upper Deck matched Score by including a Canadian National Junior Championship subset (featuring Lindros, Pat Falloon, and Scott Niedermayer, who were the top three respective picks in the 1991 NHL draft) in its high-number set.

The 1991–92 hockey card season saw a decline in the public's interest in Canadian and French versions. But overall, the hockey card market enjoyed further growth, at least in the area of supply. All seven major 1990–91 sets returned, and four new "premium" sets made their debuts: Pro Set Platinum, Parkhurst (also produced by Pro Set), Score Pinnacle, and Topps Stadium Club. Overall, the values of the new sets generally remained stable or decreased because of overproduction.

The 1992–93 hockey card season will be remembered for two things: the pervasiveness of insert card sets, and the come-from-behind success of Bowman. The five returning licensees joined with newcomer Fleer to produce twelve regular sets and a staggering thirty-one insert sets. In reaction to the overproduction of the preceding years, Topps drastically curtailed its shipments of Bowman hockey. This reduction of supply, along with the production of a number of short-printed insert cards, made the set wildly popular with collectors, and signaled the start of a new direction in card manufacturing.

The 1993–94 season was drastically affected by the NHL and NHLPA's joint decision to limit licensees to two brands each. The new regulations were particularly tough on Topps, which released five sets in 1992–93 (including two through sub-licensee OPC). The company responded by dropping both base products and the Bowman line, leaving only Stadium Club, Topps, and OPC Premier. After experiencing financial troubles, Pro Set was denied a new license. The rights to the Parkhurst brand, which had served as Pro Set's premium product, were sold to Upper Deck, which continued the revival of the grand Parkhurst name as a super-premium line in late 1993. Upper Deck also broke with tradition by issuing its base brand set in two distinct series. And in the place of Pro Set, the NHL and NHLPA awarded the fifth license to Leaf Brands, which released a two-series, super-premium product, as well as a premium series under the Donruss imprint.

The 1994–95 card season was as memorable as the lockout that curtailed the NHL schedule to a mere forty-eight games. Collectors were given a total of sixteen separate sets from which to choose, as well as more than ninety insert issues; both were new highs for the hockey hobby. The explosion was made possible by the relaxing of the two-brand limit imposed the previous year. Companies were allowed to drop the second series of one brand each in favor of a new product. This move was made by the licensing bodies in an effort to spur sales when the season finally got underway in January 1995. The second series of Donruss, Flair, Parkhurst, Score, and Stadium Club were replaced by Leaf Limited, Fleer, SP, Select, and Finest, respectively. Upper Deck also produced a set in conjunction with the NHLPA called "Be A Player." Each pack contained one card bearing an authentic signature from an NHL player—a huge development. With so many options, single-player and team collecting became the predominant collecting styles in the hobby. Many hobbyists limited their pursuits to the various insert issues. Following the path established by the hobby in other sports, manufacturers also courted collectors with a variety of interactive inserts based on game performances, such as the Stadium Club Super Teams and Upper Deck Predictors series, and multilevel parallel and redemption issues.

In a bold marketing move aimed at gaining traction in the burgeoning European hobby segment, Upper Deck released a second Parkhurst series in 1994–95, entitled SE, solely in eleven European countries. This expansion into the European market served to alleviate any burden on the company caused by contraction on the domestic side. Of course, the most dramatic announcement of the season came in November when O-Pee-Chee, the venerable Canadian card manufacturer, revealed that the 1994–95 Series II product would be its last. The company cited declining sales, a changing marketplace, and internal goal revisions as the reasons for the change.

The 1995–96 season saw more cards produced than ever before—150 sets, including parallels. Topps declined to renew its license, and Pinnacle bought Leaf/Donruss. The most popular sets of the year were the new breed of Canadian-only inserts from Topps, Home Grown Canada, and OPC parallel, all of which benefited from the presence of short prints.

The 1996–97 season again saw a huge increase in sets produced, with parallel sets and serial numbering taking center stage. Several products had production runs limited to 150 copies or fewer per card. The big winners in this race were the Select Certified Mirror parallels; reportedly, just twenty-four copies of the Gold Mirrors were produced. While insert cards played a large role in the market, Rookie Cards began a pronounced march back to respectability, and collectors pursued such hyped prospects as Joe Thornton and Patrick Marleau with a vigor usually reserved for elite superstars.

The 1997–98 season marked the debut of Pacific Trading Cards and the finale of Pinnacle/Donruss. The latter company will always be remembered for its innovations: cards in a can (as well as parallels of the cans), cards in a tin, superb die-cut technology, stamp sets, the fusing of plastic and cardboard, the meshing of jerseys, sticks, gloves, and pads with cardboard, and many other advances. This was also the first year in which an entire base set, Pinnacle Totally Certified, was issued with serial numbers. The

1997–98 season also saw the reemergence of the Beehive line, chock-full of cards featuring young talent and veterans alike. Autograph cards also played a large part in the 1997–98 hockey card season. Upper Deck's SP Authentic led the way, with over forty different autograph cards available in boxes. In the 1998–99 season, Topps re-entered the hockey market, joining a marketplace that was rife with both variety and innovation.

The 1999–2000 season will forever be remembered as the year of the memorabilia card. All four major hockey card manufacturers (Pacific, Topps, Upper Deck, and the new Be a Player) produced numerous game jersey cards, stick cards, puck cards, and various other card-memorabilia combinations. One result of this proliferation of memorabilia cards was lower secondary market prices, which made such cards available to more of the collecting public. The season also was noteworthy as the year of the short-printed Rookie Card—a year when collectors jumped at the chance to own low-print-run, serial-numbered RCs of their favorite players.

At the 2000 National Convention, In the Game set the direction for the 2000–01 season by announcing that it would release a product featuring one memorabilia card per pack. By the time this ultra-premium product—Be A Player Ultimate Memorabilia—hit the market late in the season, three other one-per-pack memorabilia brands had already appeared on dealer shelves. And, though increased availability may have lessened the glamour of these cards, it also allowed every hobbyist—no matter what his or her budget—to enjoy them. Be A Player Ultimate Memorabilia also made news by setting a new standard in pricing, with packs selling for more than $100 a pop. Numerous products were issued with double-digit suggested retail prices—including SP Game-Used Edition, which had a price of $30 for a four-card pack. Serial-numbered Rookie Cards were also a dominant factor in the market, with each company attempting to trump the others by issuing RCs with lower and lower print runs. When the dust had settled, Be A

Player, Private Stock, and Titanium had set the standard, each producing a run of rookies limited to just ninety-nine copies. However, this plan backfired somewhat as collectors veered away from cards they couldn't possibly obtain and chose to spend their money on slightly more accessible print runs in the 1,000-copy range.

The 2001–02 season was not without its share of excitement and innovation. Pacific turned the hobby on its ear by announcing that, in Titanium hobby packs, cards featuring rookie players would be serial numbered to the individual players' jersey numbers, with one of the cards being numbered one-of-one. Though not recognized as true RCs by the hobby, these ultra-rare cards traded for record prices on the secondary market and created quite a debate among collectors. The memorabilia card craze that had started in 2000–01 also continued into this season. Upper Deck released a $100-per-pack product in UD Premier Collection, with each pack containing an autograph, a serial-numbered base card, a memorabilia card, and a serial-numbered Rookie Card. The 2001–02 season is also remembered for one of the best rookie crops of the decade. Spurred by the quality and limited quantities assured by serial numbering, Rookie Cards drove sales for many of the year's top products. Among the most popular were those featuring Ilya Kovalchuk, Pavel Datsyuk, Kristian Huselius, and Stephen Weiss. Some sets that were released too early in the season to include actual rookies offered exchange cards, which could be redeemed for cards featuring rookies who made their debuts after the product had been released. After the initial confusion sparked by this process wore off, the hobby came to accept most of these cards as true RCs.

More recently, memorabilia cards continue to be the featured attraction of many products, but the novelty of these cards has all but worn off. Widespread availability, lowered odds, and simple repetition of concepts have dulled the sheen of these former chart-toppers to the point that many featuring top stars can now be had for less than $10. Although they're still wonderful collectibles to own—after all, they contain a piece of something used by a favorite athlete—they simply don't boast the secondary market appeal they once did. The products that do maintain such appeal, however—and seemingly always will—are top Rookie Cards, certified autographs, and any other products displaying the signature innovation that has always distinguished the hockey hobby.

Top Hockey Cards

1910–1940s

1911–12 C55 Georges Vezina #38
They didn't name the NHL's best-goalie trophy after Vezina just because he had a catchy name. On the contrary, he was the game's first superstar stopper.

1933–34 OPC V304A Eddie Shore #3
The NHL's first great defenseman. As mean as they came, but the man knew how to win.

1940–41 OPC V301–2 Milt Schmidt #132
Schmidt, the leader of the famous Kraut Line in Boston, was the dominant pivot of his era.

1950s

1951–52 Parkhurst Maurice Richard #4
Richard lived up to one of the greatest nicknames in sports history: "the Rocket." He was the first man to score fifty goals in a season, and was the game's most prolific goal scorer when he retired.

1951–52 Parkhurst Doug Harvey #10
A bruising defenseman who could skate like the wind, Harvey was one of the first to play the position with some regard for offense. He won four Norris trophies and five Stanley Cups.

1951–52 Parkhurst Bernie Geoffrion #14
Regarded as the father of the slap shot, Geoffrion was the second man in NHL history to record fifty goals in a single season.

1951–52 Parkhurst Red Kelly #55
Talk about versatile: Kelly topped all defensemen in scoring six times in his career, then switched to playing center, where he helped lead the Leafs to four Stanley Cups.

1951–52 Parkhurst Ted Lindsay #56
As part of the famed Production Line, "Terrible Ted" won a scoring title, racked up 1,808 penalty minutes, and contributed to four Wings Stanley Cups.

1951–52 Parkhurst Terry Sawchuk #61
Sawchuk holds the all-time record for shutouts (103) and is second in career wins (447).

1951–52 Parkhurst Alex Delvecchio #63
Delvecchio spent his entire twenty-four-year career with the Wings, playing the third-highest number of games in NHL history, many of them centering Gordie Howe.

1951–52 Parkhurst Gordie Howe #66
Widely known as "Mr. Hockey," Howe is regarded by many as the finest player ever to play the game.

1951–52 Parkhurst Howie Meeker #72
A Calder Trophy winner in 1947, Meeker was a beloved personality on Hockey Night in Canada.

1952–53 Parkhurst George Armstrong #51
The "Chief" (as he was known for his native background) retired a four-time Stanley Cup champion after the 1970–71 season.

1952–53 Parkhurst Tim Horton #58
A fearless and effective blue-liner, Horton achieved immortality through his cross-Canada chain of donut shops.

1953–54 Parkhurst Jean Beliveau #27
"Le Gros Bill" was the epitome of skilled-yet-graceful play, and one of hockey's greatest captains.

1953–54 Parkhurst Gump Worsley #53
With a name like "Gump," it's no surprise that Worsley is remembered as one of hockey's most beloved figures. The roly-poly goalie with the red crew cut led the Habs to four Cups, and was one of the last netminders to play without a mask.

1954–55 Parkhurst Johnny Bower #65
Talk about tough: The maskless Bower stopped enough pucks with his face to earn more than 250 stitches. He's beloved in Toronto for helping the Leafs to three Cup victories.

1954–55 Parkhurst Fred Sasakamoose #82
Fred's card remains in demand thanks to his status as the first Native American to play in the NHL.

1955–56 Parkhurst Jacques Plante #50
Regarded by many as hockey's greatest and most innovative goalie, Plante was the first to wear a mask full-time in NHL play.

1957–58 Parkhurst Frank Mahovlich #T17
Nicknamed "The Big M," Mahovlich played on six Stanley Cup winning teams.

1957–58 Topps Johnny Bucyk #10
A hardworking but clean player, Bucyk enjoyed an impressive twenty-three–year career. He capped it off as the all-time top-scoring left wing, with 1,369 points.

1957–58 Topps Glenn Hall #20
"Mr. Goalie" was not only a magnificent puck stopper, but also hockey's iron man between the pipes, playing in an amazing 502 consecutive games—all without wearing a mask!

1958–59 Topps Bobby Hull #66
One of hockey's most colorful characters, Hull forever changed the face of hockey by jumping to the WHA in 1972.

1960s

1960–61 Topps Stan Mikita #14
The inventor of the curved hockey stick, or banana blade, won three scoring titles, netting 1,467 points in just 1,394 games.

1961–62 Parkhurst Dave Keon #5
One of the greatest captains in Maple Leafs history, Keon, like Beliveau, was the epitome of clean, stylish play.

1963–64 Parkhurst Alex Faulkner #42
The first player born in Newfoundland to play in the NHL.

1965–66 Topps Gerry Cheevers #31
A two-time Cup winner with the Bruins, he's even better known for his unique "stitch-face" mask.

1965–66 Topps Paul Henderson #51
Scorer of the winning goal in games six, seven, and eight of the 1972 Summit Series.

1965–66 Topps Yvan Cournoyer #76
A ten-time Cup winner with the Habs, Cournoyer was one of the greatest Flying Frenchmen.

1965–66 Topps Phil Esposito #116
One of the greatest goal scorers in NHL history, Esposito set the single-season mark at seventy-six in 1971–72.

1966–67 Topps Bobby Orr #35
The best defenseman of all time, and arguably the best all-around player ever.

1967–68 Topps Derek Sanderson #33
A player whose popularity exceeded his on-ice performance, Sanderson's RC is one of the hobby's most coveted.

1968–69 OPC Bernie Parent #89
He led the Flyers to two Cups in the mid-1970s, and was one of the game's greatest goalies.

1969–70 OPC Tony Esposito #138
He set the standard for shutouts in a season (fifteen), and was an inspiration to a generation of stoppers.

1970s

1970–71 OPC Brad Park #67
Playing in Orr's shadow his entire career, Park was a six-time runner-up for the Norris trophy.

1970–71 OPC Gilbert Perreault #131
The former first-overall pick was the leader of the legendary French Connection line in Buffalo.

1970–71 OPC Bobby Clarke #195
The heart and soul of the Philadelphia Flyers, Clarke is remembered as one of the toughest, grittiest, and most talented players of his generation.

1970–71 OPC Darryl Sittler #218
One of the most popular Maple Leafs of all time, Sittler will forever be remembered for the single-most-productive offensive game in NHL history, in which he logged six goals and four assists against the Bruins in 1976.

1971–72 OPC Ken Dryden #45
Dryden is regarded as one of hockey's great money goalies, winning six Cups in eight NHL seasons with Montreal.

1971–72 OPC Marcel Dionne #133
When he retired in 1989, Dionne ranked second on the NHL's all-time scoring list with 1,771 points.

1971–72 OPC Guy Lafleur #148
"The Flower" may not go down as one of the coolest nicknames ever, but Lafleur was one of hockey's most beautiful practitioners. He scored 560 career goals and won five Cups with Montreal.

1973–74 OPC Billy Smith #142
Smith came by his nickname, "Battlin' Billy," honestly. He was a ferociously competitive puck stopper who guarded his net with the zeal of a samurai. He earned four Cup rings with the Islanders.

1973–74 OPC Larry Robinson #237
The linchpin of Montreal's famed Big Three, Robinson brought a masterful blend of size and skill to the rink. He earned two Norris trophies and six season-ending All-Star nods.

1974–75 OPC Don Cherry #161
Cherry, the former coach of the Bruins and Rockies and a commentator on Hockey Night in Canada, may rank as that country's most popular personality.

1974–75 OPC Scotty Bowman #261
Bowman guided three teams to the Cup (Montreal, Pittsburgh, and Detroit) and retired as the winningest coach in NHL history with 1,244 wins.

1976–77 OPC Bryan Trottier #115
Trottier epitomized the role of the all-around center. Always dangerous with the puck (as evidenced by his 1,425 career points), he was equally gifted at shutting down the other team's best players. He won four Cups with the Isles and two more with the Penguins.

1978–79 OPC Mike Bossy #115
A marvelously gifted sniper, Bossy lit the lamp at least fifty times in each of his nine full NHL seasons and was a vital contributor to four Cup championships with the Islanders.

1979–80 OPC Wayne Gretzky #18
Gretzky was the greatest scorer in hockey history (2,857 points), and remains the most popular player with card collectors several years into his retirement.

1980s

1980–81 OPC Ray Bourque #140
The finest all-around defenseman of his era, Bourque won five Norris trophies and was a First Team All-Star thirteen times in his career.

1980–81 OPC Mark Messier #289
In the annals of the sport, Messier is regarded as one of its greatest leaders, having guided six teams to Stanley Cup glory. He also ranks as the second greatest player of all time in both points scored and games played.

1981–82 OPC Paul Coffey #11
A marvelously gifted offensive defenseman, Coffey holds the career record for blue-liner scoring (1,531 points).

1984–85 OPC Steve Yzerman #67
The second-greatest player (after Gordie Howe) to don Detroit's winged wheel, Yzerman is one of the game's greatest heroes and most gifted offensive performers. An outstanding leader, he'll be remembered as one of the hobby's favorite players.

1984–85 OPC Cam Neely #327
This former Bruins great defined the position of power forward. No player before or since has scored, hit, and fought with equal ease.

1985–86 OPC Mario Lemieux #9
If Gretzky was the game's most lethal offensive weapon, Lemieux didn't trail by much. No player has ever been blessed with the size, speed, creativity, and finish of "Le Magnifique."

1986–87 OPC Patrick Roy #53
Arguably the greatest goaltender of all time, Roy set the NHL standards for wins in the regular season (551), wins in the playoffs (151), and shutouts in the playoffs (23).

1987–88 OPC Luc Robitaille #42
Robitaille recently became the highest-scoring left wing in league history, and netted forty or more goals in each of his first eight seasons—despite having been overlooked in his draft year until the ninth round.

1988–89 OPC Brett Hull #66
Hull ranks as one of hockey's greatest snipers, having posted three seasons of seventy or more goals—including eighty-six goals in the 1990–91 season, the third-highest total ever. He currently ranks third on the all-time goals list.

1989–90 Topps Joe Sakic #113
Like Steve Yzerman, Sakic is the ultimate team player. Offensively gifted in ways of which others can only dream, he is also a proven leader, having helped Colorado to two Stanley Cup titles.

1990s

1990–91 OPC Premier Sergei Fedorov #30
Fedorov was a force in Detroit for more than a decade, playing a major role in its three Cup wins during the 1990s and early 2000s.

1990–91 OPC Premier Jaromir Jagr #50
Jagr burst onto the scene with a combination of speed, strength, and scoring rarely seen before, and has lived up to his promise by capturing five Art Ross trophies.

1990–91 Score Martin Brodeur #439
Barring a career-ending injury, Brodeur should break most of Patrick Roy's goalie records to become the best goaltender of his time.

1990–91 Upper Deck Mike Modano #46
The second American-born player to be selected first in the NHL Entry Draft, Modano has been the face of the franchise for the Minnesota/Dallas Stars since the early 1990s.

1990–91 Upper Deck Pavel Bure #526
Though this set is chock-full of HOF-caliber players, the "Russian Rocket" may be the most offensively gifted. So far,

he's racked up a Calder, two Richard trophies, and a couple of 100-point seasons.

1991–92 Pinnacle Nicklas Lidstrom #320
Probably the best two-way defenseman in the league today, Lidstrom boasts an impressive string of three straight Norris trophies, and he remains a perennial candidate. He also earned a Conn Smythe Trophy for being the most valuable player in the 2002 Stanley Cup finals.

1991–92 Upper Deck Peter Forsberg #64
One of the best playmakers ever to wear an NHL sweater, Forsberg is a surefire Hall of Famer who boasts two Stanley Cup rings and a couple of 100-point seasons in his career. He is generally regarded as the best player in the game today.

1991–92 Upper Deck Dominik Hasek #335
A five-time winner of the Vezina trophy and one of the most dynamic players of his era, Hasek also was awarded the Pearson and Hart trophies twice.

1994–95 SP Jarome Iginla #181
An awesome combination of raging-bull power and baby-soft hands, Iginla won the Richard, Hart, and Art Ross trophies for his efforts in the 2001–02 season, and shared the Richard trophy (awarded to the league's top goal scorer) in 2003–04.

1995–96 Upper Deck Jose Theodore #530
A common practice for card makers at the time, this card depicts Theodore after leading Team Canada to a gold medal at the 1996 World Junior Championships. Jose lived up to his promise in the NHL with a Vezina Trophy and a Hart trophy in 2001–02.

1996–97 Black Diamond Joe Thornton #160
Big Joe's Rookie Card is among the toughest to find in Mint condition thanks to foil details, black borders, and an unannounced print run believed to be less than 500 copies.

1997–98 Donruss Preferred Marian Hossa #162
Silver foil stock makes this single susceptible to chipping, which has resulted in short supplies of Mint copies.

1997–98 Zenith Vincent Lecavalier #95
This innovative set begged the question: Did collectors dare to tear? By inserting regular-sized cards "inside" oversized cards that had to be cut open to reveal their smaller counterparts, a limited supply of base rookies was assured.

1998–99 SP Authentic Milan Hejduk #95
The first set with a serial-numbered print run for rookies (2,000 copies), this is the best RC featuring the Avalanche sniper.

1999–2000 SPx Pavel Brendl #166
Part of the first set to include certified autographs of rookie players on its Rookie Cards, this single featured one of the hottest prospects of its time.

2000S

2000–01 Black Diamond Dany Heatley #63
Though super-prospect Heatley was still playing with the University of Wisconsin at the time, a licensing agreement with Team Canada allowed Upper Deck to produce his Rookie Card several years before he made it to the NHL.

2000–01 SPx Andrew Raycroft #121
This card was part of the first set to add swatches of game-used jerseys to cards featuring first-year players and prospects.

2000–01 Titanium Marian Gaborik #126
Pacific went out on a limb by limiting Rookie Cards in the set to ninety-nine serial-numbered copies each, the shortest print run in history.

2000–01 Upper Deck Ice Rick DiPietro #94
Following a stellar collegiate career, DiPietro was the first goalie to be selected first overall in the NHL draft. This card was available only in an "update" product (the first of its kind), which contained RCs of players making their debuts late in the season.

2001–02 Titanium Draft Day Edition Stephen Weiss #133
In 2001–02, the NHLPA set guidelines that restricted card companies from producing Rookie Cards for players first appearing in the NHL after March 30. Weiss made his debut just before the deadline, and was included in just five sets his rookie year.

2001–02 UD Premier Collection Ilya Kovalchuk #109
Being selected first overall in the NHL draft has proved to be just the tip of the iceberg for this gifted Russian sniper. Kovalchuk came in second in the Calder race his first year in the league at the age of 18, and forged a three-way tie for the Richard trophy during the 2003–04 season. At $100 suggested retail per pack, this set created a different pricing standard for Rookie Cards.

2002–03 UD Premier Collection Rick Nash #80
The combination of a certified autograph and a game-worn jersey patch makes this 2003–04 Richard trophy winner's RC his most expensive—and at just ninety-nine copies, one of his most limited.

2003–04 Private Stock Reserve Marc-Andre Fleury #134
One of the most highly touted prospects to come out of Que-

bec in several years, Fleury is being looked to in the net as the hope for the Penguins' future. Though he struggled his first season, Fleury should rebound nicely with more seasoning, and should backstop Pittsburgh back to glory.

2003–04 SP Authentic Jordin Tootoo #148
The first Inuit ever to be drafted and play in the NHL, Tootoo looks to make an impact every night by throwing his body around and being physical. He's quickly become a fan favorite.

2005–06 The Cup Alexander Ovechkin #179
Crosby's equal on the ice isn't quite his equal in the hobby, except for this single. Thanks to the availability of more multi-color patch swatches, Ovechkin's Cup RC can match Crosby's $5,000 pull.

2005–06 The Cup Sidney Crosby #180
Crosby, the most anticipated freshman since Mario Lemieux, delivered on the hype with a monster first season. All of his RCs are hobby gems, but this is the one that redefined the market for hockey rookies. Limited to 99 copies and augmented by a patch swatch and autograph, it instantly commanded prices in excess of $5,000.

10

THE HISTORY OF BASKETBALL CARDS

The earliest known basketball collectibles are team postcards issued at the turn of the 20th century. Many of these postcards feature collegiate or high school teams of the day. Postcards were intermittently issued throughout the first half of the 20th century, with the bulk of them coming out in the 1920s and 1930s. Unfortunately, the cataloging of these collectibles was sporadic at best. In addition, many collectors regard these postcards more as memorabilia than as trading cards.

In 1910, College Athlete Felts (catalog number B-33) made their debut. These felts, made of cotton flannel fabric, depicted college athletes competing in various sports. Of a total of 270 felts, twenty featured basketball players.

The first true basketball trading cards were issued by Murad Cigarettes in 1911. The "College Series" cards depict a number of sports and colleges, including four college basketball teams (Luther, Northwestern, Williams, and Xavier). In addition to these small (2 x 3–inch) cards, Murad issued a large (8 x 5–inch) basketball card featuring Williams College (catalog number T-6) as part of another multisport set.

The first basketball cards ever to be issued in gum packs were distributed in 1933 by Goudey in its aforementioned multisport Sport Kings set, which was the first issue to list individual and professional players. Four cards from the complete forty-eight-card set feature original Celtics basketball players Nat Holman, Ed Wachter, Joe Lapchick, and Eddie Burke.

The growth of the NBA from 1948 to 1951 sparked an initial boom, both for the sport of basketball and the cards that chronicled it. In 1948, Bowman created the first trading-card set exclusively devoted to basketball, thus ushering in the modern era of hoops collectibles. This seventy-two-card Bowman set includes Hall-of-Famer George Mikan's Rookie Card, one of the most valuable and important basketball cards in the hobby. Mikan, pro basketball's first dominant big man, set the stage for Bill Russell, Wilt Chamberlain, and all the other legendary centers who have played the game since. In addition to the Bowman release, Topps included eleven basketball cards in its 252-card, multisport 1948 Magic Photo set. Five of the cards feature individual players (including collegiate great "Easy" Ed Macauley), another five feature colleges, and one additional card highlights a Manhattan-Dartmouth game. These eleven cards represent Topps's first effort to produce basketball trading cards. In 1948, Kellogg's also created an eighteen-card multisport set of trading cards that were inserted into boxes of Pep cereal. The only basketball card in the set features Mikan.

Throughout 1948 and 1949, the Exhibit Supply Company of Chicago issued oversized thick-stock multisport series in conjunction with the 1948 Olympic games. Six basketball players were featured, including Hall of Famers Mikan and Joe Fulks, among others. The cards were distributed through penny arcade machines.

From 1950 to 1951, Scott's Chips issued a thirteen-card set featuring the Minneapolis Lakers. The cards were issued in Scott's Potato and Cheese Potato Chip boxes. The cards are extremely scarce today, because many were redeemed during the 1950–51 season in exchange for game tickets and signed team pictures. This set contains possibly the scarcest Mikan issue in existence.

In 1951, the Philadelphia-based meat company Berk Ross issued a four-series, seventy-two-card multisport set. The set contains five different basketball cards, including the first cards featuring Hall of Famers Bob Cousy and Bill Sharman. Wheaties issued an oversized six-card multisport set on the backs of its cereal boxes in 1951. The only basketball player featured in this set is Mikan.

In 1952, Wheaties expanded its cereal box set to thirty cards, including six issues featuring basketball players of the day. Of these six cards, two feature Mikan (a portrait and an action shot). The 1952 cards are significantly smaller than the previous year's issue. That same year, the thirty-two-card Bread for Health set was issued. This set was one of the few trading card issues of the decade that was exclusively devoted to basketball. The cards formed the end labels of bread packages, and were probably meant to be housed in albums. This set was issued by Fisher's Bread in the New Jersey, New York, and Pennsylvania areas, and by NBC Bread in the Michigan area; such limited distribution has ensured that it remains exceedingly rare.

One must skip ahead to the 1957–58 season to find the next major basketball issue, again produced by Topps. Its eighty-card basketball set from that year is recognized within the hobby as the second major modern basketball issue. This set included Rookie Cards featuring all-time greats such as Bill Russell, Bob Cousy, and Bob Pettit.

In 1960, Post cereal created a nine-card multisport set, devoting most of the backs of its cereal boxes to full-color picture frames of the athletes. Hall-of-Famers Cousy and Pettit are the two featured basketball players.

For the 1961–62 season, Fleer issued the third major modern basketball set. The sixty-six-card set contains the Rookie Cards of all-time greats such as Wilt Chamberlain, Oscar Robertson, and Jerry West. That same year, Bell Brand Potato Chips inserted trading cards (one per bag) featuring that year's L.A. Lakers, including scarce early issues of Hall-of-Famers West and Elgin Baylor.

Although there were no major basketball card sets released from 1963 to 1968, Topps printed a very limited quantity of standard-size black-and-white test issue cards in 1968, prior to its nationwide return to the basketball card market during the 1969–70 season. The 1969–70 Topps set began a thirteen-year run of production that ended in 1981–82. This was about the time at which the league's popularity bottomed out—and before it began its ascent to the lofty levels of today.

Topps's prolific production run includes several sets that are troublesome for today's collectors. For example, the 1969–70, 1970–71, and 1976–77 sets are larger than standard size, thus making them hard to store and preserve. In addition, the 1980–81 set consists of standard-size panels containing three cards each. Completing and cataloging this set (which features the classic Larry Bird RC/Magic Johnson RC/Julius Erving panel) is challenging, to say the least.

The Star Company emerged in 1983 to fill the basketball card void, issuing three attractive sets of basketball cards along with a plethora of peripheral sets. Star's 1983–84 premiere offering was issued in four groups. The first series (cards 1–100) can be very difficult to obtain, because many of the early team subsets were miscut and destroyed before release. The 1984–85 and 1985–86 sets were more widely and evenly distributed.

Even so, cards representing players' initial appearances on any of the three Star Company sets are considered Extended Rookie Cards—not regular Rookie Cards—because of the relatively limited distribution. Most notable among these cards is Michael Jordan's 1984–85 Star XRC, the most valuable sports card issued in a 1980s set.

In 1986, Fleer took over the right to produce cards for the NBA. Its 1986–87, 1987–88, and 1988–89 sets each contain 132 attractive, colorful cards depicting mostly stars and superstars. These sets were sold in the familiar wax-pack format, with twelve cards and one sticker per pack. Fleer increased its set size to 168 in 1989–90, and was joined by NBA Hoops, which produced a 300-card first series (containing David Robinson's only Rookie Card) and a fifty-two-card second series. The demand for all three Star Company sets, along with the first four Fleer sets and the premiere NBA Hoops set, skyrocketed during the early part of 1990.

The basketball card market stabilized somewhat from 1990 to 1991, with both Fleer and Hoops stepping up production tremendously. A new major set, SkyBox, also made a splash in the market with its unique "high-tech" cards featuring computer-generated backgrounds. Because of overproduction, none of the three major 1990–91 sets experienced value growth, although the increased competition led to higher quality and more innovative products. Another milestone of the 1990–91 season was the first-time inclusion of current rookies in update sets (NBA Hoops, SkyBox Series II, and Fleer Update). The NBA Hoops and SkyBox issues feature the season's eleven lottery picks, while Fleer's 100-card boxed set features all rookies of any significance. In an effort to fill the draft-pick niche, the small company Star Pics (not to be confused with Star Company) printed a seventy-card set in late 1990, but because the set was not licensed by the NBA most collectors do not consider it a major set. The set does, however, contain the first nationally distributed cards featuring 1990–91 rookies Derrick Coleman and Kendall Gill, among others.

1992 Upper Deck Shaquille O'Neal RC #1

In 1991–92, the draft-pick market pioneered by Star Pics expanded to include several competitors. More significantly, that season saw releases from the three established NBA card brands, plus Upper Deck, which was known throughout the hobby for its high-quality card stock and photography. Upper Deck's first basketball set arguably captured NBA action better than any previous set. But its value—like that of all other major 1990–91 and 1991–92 NBA sets—declined because of overproduction. On the bright side, the historic entrance of NBA players into Olympic competition kept interest in basketball cards alive long after the Chicago Bulls won their second straight NBA championship. So for at least one year, the basketball card market—probably the most seasonal of the four major sports card markets—remained in the spotlight for an extended period of time.

The 1992–93 season will be remembered as the year of Shaq—the debut season of the most heralded rookie in many years. Shaquille O'Neal headlined the most promising rookie class in NBA history, sparking unprecedented interest in basketball cards. Among O'Neal's many talented rookie companions were Alonzo Mourning, Jim Jackson, and Latrell Sprewell. Classic Games, known primarily for producing draft-pick and minor-league-baseball cards, shocked the hobby by signing O'Neal to an exclusive contract through 1992, thus delaying the appearances of O'Neal's NBA-licensed cards. Shaquille's Classic and NBA cards, particularly the inserts, became some of the most sought-after collectibles in years. As a direct result of O'Neal and his fellow rookie standouts, the basketball card market achieved a new level of popularity in 1993.

In 1994–95, the return of Michael Jordan from retirement, coupled with the high-impact splash of Detroit Pistons rookie Grant Hill, kept collector interest high. In addition, the NBA granted all licensed manufacturers the opportunity to create a fourth brand of basketball cards that year, allowing each to create a selection of clearly defined niche products at different price points. The manufacturers also expanded their calendar release dates, with 1994–95 cards released on a consistent basis from August 1994 all the way through June 1995. The super-premium card market expanded greatly as the battle for the best selling $5 (or more) pack reached epic levels by season's end.

The collecting year of 1996–97 brought even more to the table, with a prominent group of tough parallel sets and an influx of autographs available at lower ratio pulls. One of the greatest rookie classes in some time also positively impacted the collecting season, with players such as Allen Iverson, Kobe Bryant, and Steve Nash showing great promise. Topps Chrome, an exciting card brand featuring a metallic-chromium design, was also introduced, sparking a rookie frenzy not seen since the days of the 1986–87 Fleer set.

In 1997–98, Kobe Bryant was deemed the next Michael Jordan, and his cards escalated in value throughout the year. Autographs and serial-numbered inserts were the key inserts to chase. Many of these products featured low numbering; some were even one-of-one.

The 1998–99 season saw huge changes in basketball collecting, as the players' strike crushed a growing market and sent manufacturers scrambling. On top of this, Jordan decided to retire (again), thus dealing another direct blow to the hobby. Many releases were cut back or canceled altogether. However, there was a bright spot once the season began: a great rookie class led by Vince Carter. The hobby was able to take advantage of this class by creating shorter-print-run products that featured its many promising players.

The 1999–2000 season was one of transition. Vince Carter became the new hobby hero, the NBA-champion Lakers helped buoy the hobby thanks to Bryant and O'Neal, and another solid rookie class emerged—led by Steve Francis and Elton Brand, who shared Rookie-of-the-Year honors. The 1999–2000 card releases all combined elements of short-printed or serially numbered rookies, autographs, and game-worn materials.

The 2000–01 season will definitely leave its mark on the face of the hobby for years to come. Noteworthy releases include the first one-per-pack graded insert in Upper Deck Ultimate Collection, the first one-per-pack memorabilia release in SP Game Floor, and the first one-per-box autographed jersey in Fleer Legacy. Rookie Cards were all the rage and were available in several formats and pricing tiers.

The 2001–02 release season continued the trends of previous seasons, with nearly every set issued featuring some type of memorabilia and/or autographed element. Moreover, Jordan created a frenzy within the hobby when he rose up out of retirement as a mentor and player for the young Washington Wizards squad. Base Jordan-card values (often as high as $10 to $12) dominated sets, but the explosive volume of sales provided the biggest boost as far as hobby dollars went.

The 2002–03 season paved the way for the globalization of basketball trading cards. The 2002 NBA draft boasted the highest number of foreign players (ten) to ever be selected in the first round. From the perspective of international card collecting, the biggest draw was the number one draft choice, Yao Ming. Unlike most big men drafted, Ming had the ability to come in right away and put up good numbers for his Houston squad. Ming and Amare Stoudemire, a high-school draftee for Phoenix, were a dynamic combination—the perfect one-two punch needed to revitalize a hobby that was slowly dying after the retirement (again) of Jordan in 1997. Though the number of products released during the 2002–03 season was lower than in previous years, manufacturers rein-

vested in better-looking cards and more quality products. The move paid off.

1957–58 Topps Bill Russell #77

Today, the basketball hobby continues to gain steam, buoyed immeasurably by the Jordan-like premieres of high-school phenoms LeBron James and Carmelo Anthony, both of whom entered the NBA during the 2003–04 season. Together, James and Anthony revitalized the NBA trading card market and, in essence, benefited the entire trading card industry by sending fans en masse to hobby shops across the country.

1961–62 Fleer Wilt Chamberlain #8

Top Basketball Cards

1940s

1948 Bowman George Mikan #69
George Mikan is still regarded as the pioneer "big man" in the sport—which is why his is the most sought-after Rookie Card in the set. This 1948 Bowman is accepted by the hobby as the first mainstream card issue.

1950s

1957–58 Topps Bob Cousy #17
Cousy's flashy style of play made him an instant fan favorite, and playing in Boston—which has always been one of basketball's hotbeds—further increased his popularity. Mint versions of 1957–58 Topps cards are difficult to come by, so they fetch large premiums.

1957–58 Topps Bill Russell #77
Bill Russell is hailed as one of the game's greatest defensive players. Primarily known for his shot blocking, Russell was

one of the earliest players to bring the game "above the rim."

1960s

1961–62 Fleer Wilt Chamberlain #8
Basketball experts still regard "the Stilt" as the most dominating player in NBA history. To date, Chamberlain is the only player to have scored 100 points in a single game. The original price of 1961–62 Fleer packs was five cents; Chamberlain's card now sells for $500–$900.

1961–62 Fleer Jerry West #43
A ball-dribbling Jerry West is possibly the most recognized image in basketball: It's West's silhouette that appears on the NBA logo.

1970–71 Topps Pete Maravich #123

1969–70 Topps Lew Alcindor #25
Alcindor later changed his name to Kareem Abdul-Jabbar and racked up six championships, six MVP awards, and nineteen All-Star appearances, and retired as the game's leading scorer (38,387 points) and shot blocker (3,189).

1970s

1970–71 Topps Pete Maravich #123
At a time when behind-the-back passes were few and far between, "Pistol Pete" was not only making them . . . he was faking them.

1972–73 Topps Julius Erving #195
"Dr. J" and several other ABA high-flyers introduced the world to the slam dunk. Erving's persona both on and off the court has earned him a reputation as the NBA's model spokesman.

1974–75 Topps Bill Walton #39
One of basketball's great coaches, Dr. Jack Ramsay, said that Bill Walton was both the greatest player and greatest man he's ever coached. Walton is still heavily involved with the NBA as both a writer and a commentator.

1980s

1980–81 Topps Larry Bird/Julius Erving/Magic Johnson #6
Perhaps the most influential card of the early 1980s features Bird and Magic, who had already developed a famous rivalry during college. Though both are featured on several other player combinations in the set, this is their only true Rookie Card; when collectors dig for Bird and Magic RCs, this is the card they want.

1986–87 Fleer Charles Barkley #7

1986–87 Fleer Clyde Drexler #26

1986–87 Fleer Patrick Ewing #32

1986–87 Fleer Michael Jordan #57

1986–87 Fleer Karl Malone #68

1986–87 Fleer Hakeem Olajuwon #82

1986–87 Fleer Isiah Thomas #109

1986–87 Fleer Dominique Wilkins #121

The 1986–87 Fleer set is widely considered to be the first modern-era basketball card set, and is the basketball card hobby's definitive release. The last issue from a major manufacturer had been produced by Topps in 1981–82; so when the Fleer set hit the street, it picked up all RC designations for players who had joined the league during that four-year card hiatus. Card #57, Michael Jordan's RC, is possibly the most recognizable and sought after of all basketball cards. Collectors are constantly submitting the Jordan RC for grading, and the highest price assigned to a graded basketball card is $100,000—for the first graded BGS pristine 10 card to hit the market.

No set to date has crammed this many big name RCs into a single product. Though prices of some single cards have leveled off over time, mint-condition sealed packs sell for upwards of $400, and complete boxes (containing thirty-six packs) are valued in the $15,000 range.

1989–90 Hoops David Robinson #138
The 1989–90 Hoops release was the first basketball release to dominate the entire sports card market, mostly because of this Robinson RC. The years 1990–98 were the most popular and lucrative years for basketball cards, and this set—the first to demonstrate the hobby's mass-market appeal—started it all.

1990s

1992–93 Hoops Magic's All-Rookies Shaquille O'Neal #1
The first Magic's All-Rookies installment began the insert card craze that gripped the hobby for much of the early and mid-1990s. In particular, the hype surrounding Shaq brought the hobby to new heights. Shaq also made many appearances in draft sets by the Classic company, which supplied the hobby with a wave of early Shaquille O'Neal autographed cards.

1992–93 Stadium Club Beam Team Shaquille O'Neal #21
Beam Team introduced the concept of a parallel set. In its heyday, the Shaq card traded for several hundred dollars.

Parallel sets are now a staple, and nearly every new set has some type of parallel element to it.

1992–93 Upper Deck SP Shaquille O'Neal #1
Shaq had distributors and card dealers lined up for an allocation of product; he was so popular that there simply weren't enough Shaq products to satisfy consumer demand. Ten years later, the buzz surrounding LeBron James and Carmelo Anthony in the 2003–2004 draft has been the only comparable event in terms of hype and new-product sales. This is Shaq's key RC.

1993–94 Finest Chris Webber #212
Touted as the industry's first super-premium set, this entire product was printed on foil-board. It also introduced the hobby to a well-known parallel element: the refractor. Refractors appear to be identical to base cards, but are treated with a foil process that causes them to refract light with a rainbow-like effect. Since the release of 1993–94 Finest, nearly all card manufacturers produce one or several premium sets.

1993–94 Upper Deck SE Die Cut All-Stars Shaquille O'Neal #E13
Impressive card design and player selection sparked demand for UD's SE Die Cut All-Stars. Complete sets were gathered at an alarming rate, which drove prices through the roof. This set is still attractive, and makes another successful appearance as an insert in the 2003–04 Upper Deck release.

1996 SPx Michael Jordan Autograph #NNO
The 1996 SPx release introduced collectors to Michael Jordan autographs. Over time, Jordan has signed plenty of autographs for Upper Deck (Jordan is also an Upper Deck spokesman) and is still one of the biggest draws to current UD products.

1996–97 Fleer Lucky 13 Kobe Bryant #13
As Kobe improved in the league, his cards saw phenomenal increases in value. The Kobe card was a regular on Beckett Basketball's "Hot List" for several years. The Lucky 13 set made so much money for the hobby that several different counterfeit versions are known to exist. As a result, the safest way to purchase this card is in graded form.

1996–97 Topps Chrome Kobe Bryant #138
Topps Chrome debuted low in the price guide, but climbed in value as Kobe Bryant and Allen Iverson became the hobby's two favorite sons. The popularity of Bryant and Iverson, combined with the popularity of Michael Jordan and the high-profile championship victories of the Chicago Bulls, helped raise the hobby's profile to new heights.

1998–99 SP Authentic Vince Carter RC #95
This release was the first in which Rookie Cards were produced with sequential serial numbers. At the time, 3,500 copies was considered to be a short print run (RCs numbered to as low as 99 currently exist in basketball). Carter's Rookie Card was also one of the first big dollar cards when the concept of grading was introduced.

2003–04 SPx
LeBron James
#151

2000S

2000–01 SPx Darius Miles #133
Though Miles has been a background player for most of his career, he joined the league with so much promise that a BGS 9.5 Gem Mint Darius card sold for $25,000. As of the 2005–06 season, Miles has been a disappointment—but at the time, the graded sale of his card was the largest in history.

2002–03 SPx Yao Ming #132
Though not his most valuable Rookie Card, this SPx card is still one of Ming's most popular because it combines both a game-worn jersey and an autograph. The globalization of basketball has been attributed to the original 1992 USA Olympic Dream Team; however, it's Yao who has opened the door to the globalization of basketball collectibles and merchandise.

2003–04 SPx LeBron James #151
To date, this is LeBron James's key Rookie Card.

2003–04 SPx Carmelo Anthony #153
How can we throw LeBron's name out there without also mentioning Carmelo? Though the hype surrounding LeBron would have served the industry fine on its own, another promising prospect named Carmelo Anthony provided the icing on the cake. SPx brings us Melo's key Rookie Card.

2003–04 UD Top Prospects Signs of Success LeBron James #SSLJ
When LeBron joined the NBA, he brought with him a level of hype that had never before been seen. This made 2003–04 a remarkably profitable year for collecting—not only in terms of money, but in terms of rejuvenated interest in the sport and new collectors brought on board. Not since Shaquille O'Neal has an undrafted player become a household name. This Signs of Success autographed card was the first LeBron 'graph to hit the open market.

2004–05 Exquisite Collection Dwight Howard JSY AU RC #90
Howard is the most polished young big man in the game today. At only 20 years old, his growth potential both on the court and in the hobby is limitless.

2005–06 Exquisite Collection Chris Paul JSY AU RC #46
Built like Allen Iverson, yet only more explosive, Paul is the hobby's newest point guard darling.

Part 3
RESOURCE GUIDE

MUSEUMS, ASSOCIATIONS, AND ORGANIZATIONS

National Baseball Hall of Fame and Museum
25 Main Street
Cooperstown, NY 13326
(607) 547–7200 or toll-free (888) 425–5633
www.baseballhalloffame.org

Pro Football Hall of Fame
2121 George Halas Drive NW
Canton, OH 44708
(330) 456–8207
www.profootballhof.com

Naismith Memorial Basketball Hall of Fame
1000 West Columbus Avenue
Springfield, MA 01105
(413) 781–6500 or toll-free (877)4HOOPLA
www.hoophall.com

Hockey Hall of Fame
BCE Place
30 Yonge Street
Toronto, ON
M5E 1X8
Canada
(416) 360–7735
www.hhof.com

College Football Hall of Fame
111 South St. Joseph Street
South Bend, IN 46601
(574) 235–9999 or toll-free (800) 440–3263
www.collegefootball.org

Motorsports Hall of Fame of America
P.O. Box 194
Novi, MI 48376–0194
(800) 250–7223
www.mshf.com

International Motorsports Hall of Fame and Museum
P.O. Box 1018
Talladega, AL 35161
(256) 362–5002
www.motorsportshalloffame.com

International Tennis Hall of Fame
194 Bellevue Avenue
Newport, RI 02840
(401) 849–3990 or toll-free (800) 457–1144
www.tennisfame.com

National Soccer Hall of Fame and Museum
18 Stadium Circle
Oneonta, NY 13820
(607) 432–3351
www.soccerhall.org

International Boxing Hall of Fame
1 Hall of Fame Drive
Canastota, NY 13032
(315) 697–7095
www.ibhof.com

Canadian Football Hall of Fame and Museum
58 Jackson Street West
Hamilton, ON
L8P 1L4
Canada
(905) 528–7566
www.footballhof.com

The Canadian Baseball Hall of Fame & Museum
P.O. Box 1838
St. Marys, ON
N4X 1C2
Canada
(519) 284–1838
www.baseballhalloffame.ca

World Golf Hall of Fame
1 World Golf Place
St. Augustine, FL 32092
(904) 940–4000
www.wgv.com

United States Hockey Hall of Fame
801 Hat Trick Avenue
Eveleth, MN 55734
(218) 744–5167 or toll-free (800) 443–7825
www.ushockeyhall.com

National Women's Baseball Hall of Fame
P.O. Box 15282
Chevy Chase, MD 20825
(301) 847–0102
www.eteamz.com/hallfame

Negro Leagues Baseball Museum
1616 East 18th Street
Kansas City, MO 64108
(816) 221–1920 or toll-free (888) 221–NLBM
www.nlbm.com

Babe Ruth Birthplace and Museum
216 Emory Street
Baltimore, MD 21230
(410) 727–1539 or toll-free (888) 438–6909
www.baberuthmuseum.com

MAJOR LEAGUE BASEBALL

AMERICAN LEAGUE

Baltimore Orioles
Oriole Park at Camden Yards
333 West Camden Street
Baltimore, MD 21201
www.orioles.mlb.com

Boston Red Sox
Fenway Park
4 Yawkey Way
Boston, MA 02215
www.redsox.mlb.com

Chicago White Sox
U.S. Cellular Field
333 West 35th Street
Chicago, IL 60616
www.whitesox.mlb.com

Cleveland Indians
Jacobs Field
2401 Ontario Street
Cleveland, OH 44115
www.indians.mlb.com

Detroit Tigers
Comerica Park
2100 Woodward Avenue
Detroit, MI 48201
www.tigers.mlb.com

Kansas City Royals
Kauffman Stadium
1 Royal Way
Kansas City, MO 64141–6969
www.royals.mlb.com

Los Angeles Angels of Anaheim
Edison International Field
2000 Gene Autry Way
Anaheim, CA 92806
www.angels.mlb.com

Minnesota Twins
Hubert H. Humphrey Metrodome
34 Kirby Puckett Place
Minneapolis, MN 55415
www.twins.mlb.com

New York Yankees
Yankee Stadium
161st Street and River Avenue
Bronx, NY 10451
www.yankees.mlb.com

Oakland Athletics
McAfee Coliseum
7000 Coliseum Way
Oakland, CA 94621
www.athletics.mlb.com

Seattle Mariners
Safeco Field
P.O. Box 4100
Seattle, WA 98194
www.mariners.mlb.com

Tampa Bay Devil Rays
Tropicana Field
One Tropicana Drive
St. Petersburg, FL 33705
www.devilrays.mlb.com

Texas Rangers
Ameriquest Field in Arlington
1000 Ballpark Way
Arlington, TX 76011
www.rangers.mlb.com

Toronto Blue Jays
Rogers Centre
1 Blue Jays Way
Toronto, ON
M5V 1J1
Canada
www.bluejays.mlb.com

NATIONAL LEAGUE

Arizona Diamondbacks
Chase Field
401 East Jefferson Street
Phoenix, AZ 85001
www.diamondbacks.mlb.com

Atlanta Braves
Turner Field
755 Hank Aaron Drive
Atlanta, GA 30315
www.braves.mlb.com

Chicago Cubs
Wrigley Field
1060 West Addison Street
Chicago, IL 60613–4397
www.cubs.mlb.com

Cincinnati Reds
Great American Ball Park
100 Main Street
Cincinnati, OH 45202–4109
www.reds.mlb.com

Colorado Rockies
Coors Field
2001 Blake Street
Denver, CO 80205–2000
www.rockies.mlb.com

Florida Marlins
Dolphin Stadium
2269 Dan Marino Boulevard
Miami, FL 33056
www.marlins.mlb.com

Houston Astros
Minute Maid Park
501 Crawford
Houston, TX 77002
www.astros.mlb.com

Los Angeles Dodgers
Dodger Stadium
1000 Elysian Park Avenue
Los Angeles, CA 90012–1199
www.dodgers.mlb.com

Milwaukee Brewers
Miller Park
One Brewers Way
Milwaukee, WI 53214
www.brewers.mlb.com

New York Mets
Shea Stadium
123–01 Roosevelt Avenue
Flushing, NY 11368–1699
www.mets.mlb.com

Philadelphia Phillies
Citizens Bank Park
1 Citizens Bank Way
Philadelphia, PA 19148–5249
www.phillies.mlb.com

Pittsburgh Pirates
PNC Park
115 Federal Street
Pittsburgh, PA 15212
www.pirates.mlb.com

San Diego Padres
PETCO Park
100 Park Boulevard
San Diego, CA 92101
www.padres.mlb.com

San Francisco Giants
AT&T Park
24 Willie Mays Plaza
San Francisco, CA 94107
www.giants.mlb.com

St. Louis Cardinals
Busch Stadium
420 South 8th St.
St. Louis, MO 63102
www.cardinals.mlb.com

Washington Nationals
RFK Stadium
2400 East Capitol Street, SE
Washington, DC 20003
www.nationals.mlb.com

NATIONAL FOOTBALL LEAGUE

National Football League
280 Park Avenue
New York, NY 10017
www.nfl.com

Arizona Cardinals
1 Cardinal Drive
Glendale, AZ 85305
www.azcardinals.com

Atlanta Falcons
4400 Falcon Parkway
Flowery Branch, GA 30542
www.atlantafalcons.com

Baltimore Ravens
11001 Owings Mills Blvd.
Owings Mills, MD 21117
www.baltimoreravens.com

Buffalo Bills
One Bills Drive
Orchard Park, NY 14127–2296
www.buffalobills.com

Carolina Panthers
800 South Mint Street
Charlotte, NC 28202–1502
www.panthers.com

Chicago Bears
1000 Football Drive
Lake Forest, IL 60045
www.chicagobears.com

Cincinnati Bengals
One Paul Brown Stadium
Cincinnati, OH 45202
www.bengals.com

Cleveland Browns
76 Lou Groza Blvd.
Berea, OH 44017–0146
www.clevelandbrowns.com

Dallas Cowboys
One Cowboys Parkway
Irving, TX 75063
www.dallascowboys.com

Denver Broncos
13655 Broncos Parkway
Englewood, CO 80112
www.denverbroncos.com

Detroit Lions
222 Republic Drive
Allen Park, MI 48101
www.detroitlions.com

Green Bay Packers
1265 Lombardi Avenue
Green Bay, WI 54304
www.packers.com

Houston Texans
Two Reliant Park
Houston, TX 77054
www.houstontexans.com

Indianapolis Colts
7001 West 56th Street
Indianapolis, IN 46254
www.colts.com

Jacksonville Jaguars
One ALLTEL Stadium Place
Jacksonville, FL 32202
www.jaguars.com

Kansas City Chiefs
One Arrowhead Drive
Kansas City, MO 64129
www.kcchiefs.com

Miami Dolphins
7500 SW 30th Street
Davie, FL 33314
www.miamidolphins.com

Minnesota Vikings
9520 Viking Drive
Eden Prairie, MN 55344
www.vikings.com

New England Patriots
60 Washington Street
Foxboro, MA 02035
www.patriots.com

New Orleans Saints
5800 Airline Drive
Metairie, LA 70003
www.neworleanssaints.com

New York Giants
Giants Stadium
East Rutherford, NJ 07073
www.giants.com

New York Jets
1000 Fulton Avenue
Hempstead, NY 11550–1099
www.newyorkjets.com

Oakland Raiders
1220 Harbor Bay Parkway
Alameda, CA 94502
www.raiders.com

Philadelphia Eagles
NovaCare Complex
One NovaCare Way
Philadelphia, PA 19145
www.philadelphiaeagles.com

Pittsburgh Steelers
3400 South Water Street
Pittsburgh, PA 15203–2349
www.steelers.com

San Diego Chargers
4020 Murphy Canyon Road
San Diego, CA 92123
www.chargers.com

San Francisco 49ers
4949 Centennial Blvd.
Santa Clara, CA 95054
www.sf49ers.com

Seattle Seahawks
11220 NE 53rd Street
Kirkland, WA 98033
www.seahawks.com

St. Louis Rams
One Rams Way
St. Louis, MO 63045
www.stlouisrams.com

Tampa Bay Buccaneers
One Buccaneer Place
Tampa, FL 33607
www.buccaneers.com

Tennessee Titans
Baptist Sports Park
460 Great Circle Road
Nashville, TN 37228
www.titansonline.com

Washington Redskins
21300 Redskin Park Drive
Ashburn, VA 20147
www.redskins.com

NATIONAL BASKETBALL ASSOCIATION

National Basketball Association
Olympic Tower
645 Fifth Avenue
New York, NY 10022
www.nba.com

Atlanta Hawks
Centennial Tower
101 Marietta St. NW, Suite 1900
Atlanta, GA 30303
www.nba.com/hawks

Boston Celtics
226 Causeway Street, Fourth Floor
Boston, MA 02114–4714
www.nba.com/celtics

Charlotte Bobcats
333 East Trade Street
Charlotte, NC 28202
www.nba.com/bobcats

Chicago Bulls
1901 West Madison Street
Chicago, IL 60612–2459
www.nba.com/bulls

Cleveland Cavaliers
One Center Court
Cleveland, OH 44115–4001
www.nba.com/cavaliers

Dallas Mavericks
2500 Victory Avenue
Dallas, TX 75201
www.nba.com/mavericks

Denver Nuggets
1000 Chopper Circle
Denver, CO 80204
www.nba.com/nuggets

Detroit Pistons
4 Championship Drive
Auburn Hills MI 48326
www.nba.com/pistons

Golden State Warriors
1011 Broadway
Oakland, CA 94607
www.nba.com/warriors

Houston Rockets
1510 Polk Street
Houston, TX 77002
www.nba.com/rockets

Indiana Pacers
125 S. Pennsylvania Street
Indianapolis, IN 46204
www.nba.com/pacers

Los Angeles Clippers
Staples Center
1111 S. Figueroa Street, Suite 1100
Los Angeles, CA 90015
www.nba.com/clippers

Los Angeles Lakers
555 N. Nash Street
El Segundo, CA 90245
www.nba.com/lakers

Memphis Grizzlies
191 Beale Street
Memphis, TN 38103
www.nba.com/grizzlies

Miami Heat
American Airlines Arena
601 Biscayne Blvd.
Miami, FL 33132
www.nba.com/heat

Milwaukee Bucks
1001 N. Fourth Street
Milwaukee, WI 53203
www.nba.com/bucks

Minnesota Timberwolves
600 First Avenue North
Minneapolis, MN 55403
www.nba.com/timberwolves

New Jersey Nets
390 Murray Hill Parkway
East Rutherford, NJ 07073
www.nba.com/nets

New Orleans/Oklahoma City Hornets
Oklahoma Tower
210 Park Avenue, Suite 1850
Oklahoma City, OK 73102
www.nba.com/hornets

New York Knicks
Madison Square Garden
2 Pennsylvania Plaza
New York, NY 10121–0091
www.nba.com/knicks

Orlando Magic
8701 Maitland Summit Blvd.
Orlando, FL 32810
www.nba.com/magic

Philadelphia 76**ers**
3601 S. Broad Street
Philadelphia, PA 19148
www.nba.com/sixers

Phoenix Suns
201 E. Jefferson Street
Phoenix, AZ 85004
www.nba.com/suns

Portland Trailblazers
One Center Court
Suite 200
Portland, OR 97227
www.nba.com/blazers

Sacramento Kings
1 Sports Parkway
Sacramento, CA 95834
www.nba.com/kings

San Antonio Spurs
1 SBC Center
San Antonio, TX 78219
www.nba.com/spurs

Seattle Sonics
351 Elliott Ave. W., Suite 500
Seattle, WA 98119
www.nba.com/sonics

Toronto Raptors
Air Canada Centre
40 Bay Street, Suite 400
Toronto, ON
M5J 2X2
Canada
www.nba.com/raptors

Utah Jazz
301 W. South Temple
Salt Lake City, UT 84101
www.nba.com/jazz

Washington Wizards
Verizon Center
601 F Street, NW
Washington, DC 20004
www.nba.com/wizards

NATIONAL HOCKEY LEAGUE

National Hockey League
1251 Avenue of the Americas, 47th Floor
New York, NY 10020–1198
www.nhl.com

Anaheim Mighty Ducks
Arrowhead Pond
2695 E. Katella Avenue
Anaheim, CA 92806
www.mightyducks.com

Atlanta Thrashers
Philips Arena
1 CNN Center
Atlanta, GA 30303–2762
www.atlantathrashers.com

Boston Bruins
TD Banknorth Garden
100 Legends Way
Boston, MA 02114
www.bostonbruins.com

Buffalo Sabres
HSBC Arena
One Seymour H. Knox III Plaza
Buffalo, NY 14203–3096
www.sabres.com

Calgary Flames
Pengrowth Saddledome
P.O. Box 1540, Station M
Calgary, AB
T2P 3B9
Canada
www.calgaryflames.com

Carolina Hurricanes
RBC Center
1400 Edwards Mill Road
Raleigh, NC 27607
www.carolinahurricanes.com

Chicago Blackhawks
The United Center
1901 West Madison Street
Chicago, IL 60612
www.chicagoblackhawks.com

Colorado Avalanche
Pepsi Center
1000 Chopper Circle
Denver, CO 80204
www.coloradoavalanche.com

Columbus Blue Jackets
Nationwide Arena
200 W. Nationwide Blvd.
Columbus, OH 43215
www.bluejackets.com

Dallas Stars
American Airlines Center
2500 Victory Avenue
Dallas, TX 75201
www.dallasstars.com

Detroit Red Wings
Joe Louis Arena
600 Civic Center Drive
Detroit, MI 48226
www.detroitredwings.com

Edmonton Oilers
Rexall Place
7424 118th Avenue
Edmonton, AB
T5B 4M9
Canada
www.edmontonoilers.com

Florida Panthers
BankAtlantic Center
One Panther Parkway
Sunrise, FL 33323
www.floridapanthers.com

Los Angeles Kings
Staples Center
1111 S. Figueroa Street, Suite 3100
Los Angeles, CA 90015
www.lakings.com

Minnesota Wild
Xcel Energy Center
175 West Kellogg Blvd.
Saint Paul, MN 55102
www.wild.com

Montreal Canadiens
Bell Centre
1260 Rue Gauchetiere West
Montreal, PQ
H3B 5E8
Canada
www.canadiens.com

Nashville Predators
Gaylord Entertainment Center
501 Broadway
Nashville, TN 37201
www.nashvillepredators.com

New Jersey Devils
Continental Airlines Arena
50 State Highway 120
East Rutherford, NJ 07073
www.newjerseydevils.com

New York Islanders
Nassau Veterans Memorial Coliseum
1255 Hempstead Turnpike
Uniondale, NY 11553
www.newyorkislanders.com

New York Rangers
Madison Square Garden
2 Pennsylvania Plaza
New York, NY 10121
www.newyorkrangers.com

Ottawa Senators
Scotiabank Place
1000 Palladium Drive
Kanata, ON
K2V 1A5
Canada
www.ottawasenators.com

Philadelphia Flyers
Wachovia Center
3601 South Broad Street
Philadelphia, PA 19148
www.philadelphiaflyers.com

Phoenix Coyotes
Glendale Arena
9400 West Maryland Avenue
Glendale, AZ 85303
www.phoenixcoyotes.com

Pittsburgh Penguins
Mellon Arena
66 Mario Lemieux Place
Pittsburgh, PA 15219
www.pittsburghpenguins.com

San Jose Sharks
HP Pavilion at San Jose
525 West Santa Clara Street
San Jose, CA 95113
www.sjsharks.com

St. Louis Blues
Savvis Center
1401 Clark Avenue
St. Louis, MO 63103
www.stlouisblues.com

Tampa Bay Lightning
St. Pete Times Forum
401 Channelside Drive
Tampa, FL 33602
www.tampabaylightning.com

Toronto Maple Leafs
Air Canada Centre
40 Bay Street, Suite 300
Toronto, ON
M5J 2X2
Canada
www.mapleleafs.com

Vancouver Canucks
General Motors Place
800 Griffiths Way
Vancouver, BC
V6B 6G1
Canada
www.canucks.com

Washington Capitals
MCI Center
601 F Street, NW
Washington, DC 20004
www.washingtoncaps.com

SPORTS CARD COMPANIES

Donruss Playoff L.P.
2300 East Randol Mill
Arlington, TX 76011
(817) 983–0300
www.donruss.com

In The Game, Inc.
P.O. Box 697
Medford, NJ 08055
www.baptradingcards.com

Press Pass/RC2 Brands
9115 Harris Corners Parkway
Suite 200
Charlotte, NC 28269
(704) 942–3060
www.rc2corp.com

The Topps Company
1 Whitehall Street
New York, NY 10004–2109
(212) 376–0300
www.topps.com

Upper Deck
5909 Sea Otter Place
Carlsbad, CA 92010
(800) 873–7332
www.upperdeck.com

BOOKS AND MAGAZINES

Beckett Media
4635 McEwen Drive
Dallas, TX 75244
(972) 991–6657
www.beckett.com

Krause Publications
700 East State Street
Iola, WI 54990–0001
(715) 445–2214
www.collect.com

Trajan Publications
P.O. Box 28103 Lakeport PO
St. Catharines, ON
L2N 7P8
Canada
(905) 646–7744
www.cscmag.ca

ONLINE RESOURCES

INFORMATION, COLLECTING FORUMS, AND MESSAGE BOARDS

www.beckett.com

www.beckettpedia.com

www.bigleaguers.com

www.card-bored.com

www.cardbuzz.net

www.collect.com

www.fanspot.com

www.hobbyinsider.com

www.nflplayers.com

www.slam.ca

www.sportsology.net

BUYING, SELLING, AUCTIONS, AND MEMORABILIA

www.beckett.com

www.ebay.com

www.greyflannel.com

www.lelands.com

www.mountedmemories.com

www.naxcom.com

www.yahoo.com

SUPPLIES

www.cardboardgold.com

www.ultra-pro.com

GRADING

www.beckett.com/grading

www.krause.com

www.psacard.com

www.sgccard.com

Part 4

INSTANT
EXPERT QUIZ

1. In a 2000 eBay auction, one of Honus Wagner's famed T206 cards sold for what price?

2. Who are the two licensed trading card companies currently producing Major League Baseball trading cards?

3. Dr. James Beckett of Beckett Media fame holds a PhD in what?

4. What is the official name of America's largest trading card convention?

5. The first known baseball trading cards were packaged with what products?

6. During what year was Topps's twenty-five-year monopoly on the baseball card market broken?

7. What company is credited with starting baseball's "premium card" trend with a landmark premiere release in 1989?

8. What are the main areas of concern with respect to any counterfeit card?

9. What two companies are responsible for the industry's most widely used price guide magazines?

10. Baseball's first "bubble gum" cards were produced in 1933 by what company?

11. What term is used to describe a card with no flaws or wear?

12. What are the two most popular sources for trading cards today?

13. What common term refers to a regular-issue card from a major licensed manufacturer on which a player makes his or her first appearance?

14. What are three main areas of concern when determining a card's condition?

15. By year and name, what was the first "bubble gum" set devoted entirely to football players?

16. What two companies made landmark NFL trading card debuts in 1989?

17. What fast-food chain created a frenzy with a 1986 NFL trading card promotion?

18. What Hall of Fame basketball player appears on the most influential card in the 1948 Bowman basketball set?

19. What NBA superstar shares a Rookie Card with Magic Johnson and Julius Erving?

20. During what decade did hockey's popular Bee Hive photos make their debut?

Answers

1. More than $1.2 million

2. Topps and Upper Deck

3. Statistics

4. The National Sports Collectors Convention

5. Tobacco products

6. 1981

7. Upper Deck

8. Weight, dot pattern, and photo sharpness and feel

9. Beckett Media and Krause Publications

10. The Goudey Gum Company

11. Mint

12. The Internet and hobby shops

13. Rookie Card

14. Centering, corner wear, and creases

15. 1935 National Chicle

16. Score and Pro Set

17. McDonald's

18. George Mikan

19. Larry Bird

20. The 1930s

INDEX

Page numbers in *italics* refer to illustrations and captions.

U

Ultimate Collection, 75, 116
Ultra, 52
Ultra-PRO, 35, 37, 143
Unitas, Johnny, 91
United States Football League, 79
United States Hockey Hall of Fame, 126
Upper Deck, *vi*, 24, 141
    baseball, 5, 51–52, *52*, 55–56, 58, 73, 74
    basketball, 7, 114, *114*, 116, 120, 121
    football, 80, 81–82, 88, 89
    hockey, 95, 96, 97, 98, 99, 105–106, 107
U.S. Caramel, 61, *61*

V

Value, determining, 11–16
Very Good condition (Vg), 19–20
Vick, Michael, 82
Vintage cards, 4, 9–10

W

Wachter, Ed, 110
Wagner, Honus, 46, 47
Web sites
    for card shop locations, 24
    price guides, 32, 33, 34
    for show calendars, 27, 29

Weight scales, 40
Weiss, Stephen, 99
West, Jerry, 112
Wheaties, 111
White, Reggie, 79
Wild Card, 80
Williams College Murad basketball card, 110
Williams, Don, *28*
Williams, Ted, 8
Willis, Dontrelle, 58
Wizards of the Coast, 57
World Golf Hall of Fame, 126
World Hockey Association, 94
World Wide Gum Company, 62, 93
Wrapper redemption programs, 29–30, 49

X

XRC (extended rookie card), 22, 113

Y

York Caramel, 47
Young, Cy, 60

Z

Zeenuts Pacific League baseball cards, 47
Zenith, 106

ABOUT THE AUTHOR

Dr. James Beckett is the leading authority on sports card values in the United States. He is the author of numerous books on sports card collecting—such as the annual *Official Price Guide to Baseball Cards* (as well as *Football Cards* and *Basketball Cards*)—and is the founder and publisher of the popular Beckett monthly magazines for collectors and of Beckett.com, an online destination and community for sports collectibles enthusiasts.

Beckett earned his PhD in statistics from Southern Methodist University in 1975. Before launching Beckett Media in 1984, he served as an associate professor of statistics at Bowling Green University and as a vice president of a consulting firm in Dallas. In addition to being the author of over a dozen books, Dr. Beckett is the editor and publisher of numerous magazines on collecting the cards of many sports. He has made numerous appearances on radio and TV and has frequently been cited in national sports publications.